A Summer of Birds

The Hill Collection
Holdings of the LSU Libraries

A Summer of Birds

John James Audubon at Oakley House

Danny Heitman

LOUISIANA STATE UNIVERSITY PRESS ❧ BATON ROUGE

Published by Louisiana State University Press
Copyright © 2008 by Louisiana State University Press
All rights reserved
Manufactured in the United States of America
FIRST PRINTING

DESIGNER: *Amanda McDonald Scallan*
TYPEFACE: *Warnock Pro*
PRINTER AND BINDER: *Thomson-Shore, Inc*

Frontispiece portrait of John J. Audubon is by Jules Lion, lithograph, 1860.
Collection of the Louisiana State Museum, loan of T. P. Thompson.

Illustrations from Audubon's *Birds of America* are reproduced courtesy of
Special Collections, LSU Libraries.

Library of Congress Cataloging-in-Publication Data

Heitman, Danny, 1964–
 A summer of birds : John James Audubon at Oakley House / Danny
Heitman.
  p. cm. — (The Hill collection : holdings of the LSU libraries)
 Includes bibliographical references.
 ISBN 978-0-8071-3330-9 (cloth : alk. paper)
 1. Audubon, John James, 1785–1851—Homes and haunts—Louisiana—Oak-
ley Plantation. 2. Ornithologists—United States—Biography. 3. Animal
painters—United States—Biography. I. Title.
 QL31.A9H35 2008
 598.092—dc22
 [B]

                                                    2007042884

For my family

A place that ever was lived in is like a fire that never goes out. It flares up, it smolders for a time, it is fanned or smothered by circumstance, but its being is intact, forever fluttering within it, the result of some original ignition. Sometimes it gives out glory, sometimes its little light must be sought out to be seen, small and tender as a candle flame, but as certain.

—EUDORA WELTY
"Some Notes on River Country"

Contents

Illustrations

Following page 74

Acknowledgments

Between his birth in 1785 and his death in 1851, John James Audubon lived not one, but many lives. His work as a businessman, ornithologist, bird artist, writer, and naturalist identifies him as a man of multiple sides. *A Summer of Birds: John James Audubon at Oakley House* chronicles a brief but eventful season that Audubon spent on a Louisiana plantation—a summer that changed his life.

This book is not meant to supplant the full-scale biographies of Audubon already on the shelf. Readers who want a complete account of Audubon's life will profit by reading Shirley Streshinsky's *Audubon: Life and Art in the American Wilderness*, Richard Rhodes's *John James Audubon: The Making of an American*, and William Souder's *Under a Wild Sky: John James Audubon and the Making of "The Birds of America."* These books enlarged my thinking about Audubon and provided valuable insights into his Oakley period. A list of other helpful Audubon references appears in the bibliography at the back of this volume.

Of special note is *John James Audubon: Writings and Drawings*, a Library of America project edited by a consummate scholar, Christoph Irmscher. Irmscher's selection of Audubon's works was a constant companion during my research. Irmscher also generously agreed to read earlier drafts of *A Summer of Birds*, and his suggestions greatly improved the finished work.

Many other people enabled me to tell this story. Angèle Davis, secretary of Louisiana's Department of Culture, Recreation, and Tourism, connected me with helpful institutions under her direction, including the State Library of Louisiana, the Louisiana State Museum, and the Office of State Parks, which oversees Oakley House as part of the Audubon State Historic Site.

The dedicated and efficient staff of the Audubon State Historic Site, including site manager John R. House III, curator Tonya Nicolosi, tour guide Rachel Scharff, and interpretive rangers Judy Butler and Dennis J. Dufrene, took time away from many other responsibilities to answer my questions and accommodate site visits by Lori Waselchuk, an internationally renowned photographer whose pictures of Oakley contribute greatly to this book. Dufrene undertook an extensive review of the illustrations in Audubon's *Birds of America* to identify those with Oakley origins. I will never forget his diligence in embracing such a task while juggling so many other obligations. Also generous with their time and expertise were Keith Ouchley, Van Remsen, John O'Neill, Donna Dittman, and Matt Reonas. Anne B. Klein and Ann Stirling Weller, relatives of Audubon's host family at Oakley, the Pirries, patiently answered many questions about family history. Klein helped make the inclusion of the Pirrie family portraits in *A Summer of Birds* possible. Elisabeth Dart, president of the Friends of Oakley, was a wise and gracious guide through the history of Audubon in the Felicianas. My birding near Oakley House with Tracey Banowetz and Al and Cathy Troy greatly enriched my thinking about Audubon's relationship with birds.

Thomas Lanham of the Louisiana State Museum and Thomas Gresham of the Department of Wildlife and Fisheries shared pictures from their respective collections. Erik Baka, also with the Department of Wildlife and Fisheries, was of great assistance in identifying illustrations for the book. David Norwood's map of Oakley and its environs is a wonderful complement to the other illustrations.

For readers of *A Summer of Birds,* my debt to Louisiana State University's Hill Memorial Library will quickly become evident. The library boasts one of the most impressive collections of Audubon's bird pictures in the country. Without the tireless assistance and technical expertise of Elaine B. Smyth, head of Special Collections, this book would not have been possible.

Margaret Hart of LSU Press was a champion of *A Summer of Birds* from its inception, and her keen editorial guidance helped make the project a reality. Linda Lightfoot and Carl Redman, my editors at *The Advo-*

cate in Baton Rouge, granted me much-needed flexibility and encouragement while I was writing the book. Judy Jumonville and her staff of librarians at *The Advocate* helped connect me with a wealth of Audubon resources. While I was writing *A Summer of Birds,* my late friend and fellow writer, Laurie Smith Anderson, offered me a daily standard of what a writer should be.

Although many expert voices appear in *A Summer of Birds,* any errors of fact or omission are, of course, my responsibility. To study the life of John James Audubon is to be reminded that he could not have accomplished what he did without the support of his wife and children. I thought about this a great deal as my wife, Catherine, and our children, Eve and Will, adjusted their lives to accommodate my research and writing. I owe them a debt I can never repay.

A Note on Audubon's Writings

John James Audubon was not only an accomplished artist, but an observant and prolific writer. His writing is particularly important to the story of his stay at Oakley House, providing the only surviving record, however imperfect, of what happened during his Oakley period in the summer of 1821. Audubon wrote with great flair and colorful detail, but English was his second language, and his command of spelling and grammar was erratic, to say the least.

Audubon's idiosyncratic syntax has been a challenge to those who write about him. Many books about Audubon, including this one, have changed his spelling, grammar, and capitalization to make his prose more easily understandable for general readers. Not everyone is a fan of this approach. In "Audubon the Writer," noted Audubon scholar Christoph Irmscher eloquently argues that correcting Audubon's prose can flatten the flavor of his writing, and that "the less we mess with the original Audubon the better." Those who want a fuller exploration of Irmscher's views on the subject will be rewarded by reading the complete paper, available online at http://www.audubonoctavos.com/SITE/pages/ Irmscher.html. When Irmscher edited the Library of America's *John James Audubon: Writings and Drawings,* he retained Audubon's original spelling and grammar. In quoting from *Writings and Drawings,* I have followed my book's general scheme of changing misspellings and grammatical oddities in the interest of clarity.

A Summer of Birds

Bird-watching, like all other forms of pursuit, has a lot of near-misses. Hearing a wistful trill, or glimpsing a flurry of feathers from the corner of his eye, the observer pivots in the direction of his prize, only to find an empty branch still trembling like an arrow fresh from its quill. A sense of narrowly eluded encounter also touches Oakley House, a plantation home in Louisiana's West Feliciana Parish where the legendary bird artist John James Audubon lived from June through October of 1821, and now operated as a historical site by the state of Louisiana. Though Audubon left Oakley nearly two centuries ago, it can seem to the visitor as if the renowned artist has just slipped out the door.

Audubon's memory looms large at Oakley because he did big things during his stay. Summer beckons us all with its promise of discovery. For Audubon, the summer of 1821 would be just such a season of eye-opening experiences—indeed, one of the most formative summers of his life.

Audubon's life was on a hinge when he walked to the door of Oakley House, near the Louisiana community of St. Francisville, in June of 1821. The effect of that summer on Audubon reminds us of what David McCullough has said about the intrigue of history. History is interesting, said McCullough, because things did not have to turn out the way they did. They might have gone the other way.

In 1821, Audubon was at just such a turning point. An aspiring bird artist since childhood, he had sketched and painted American birds as a sideline to his real occupation, that of a prosperous Kentucky merchant. But a national economic slump in 1819 had destroyed Audubon's business, a tragic turn of events that was also oddly liberating. With his store and fledgling mill operation bankrupted, Audubon believed that financially, at least, he had little else to lose. Freed from the constraints of the merchant and mill trade, a livelihood for which he had been groomed by his businessman father, the thirty-six-year-old Audubon felt at greater liberty to pursue the art that had always been his true passion.

Thus began Audubon's odyssey to document the birds of an America still covered in woodland, but which was rapidly giving way to expanding settlement. The impoverished Audubon set out, like a biblical prophet wandering the wilderness, to paint as many birds as he could locate and compile his findings into *The Birds of America*, his ambitious omnibus of American ornithology.

It was an audacious task, and even Audubon, who had a high opinion of his own genius, suffered inevitable doubts. Money entered into his anxiety. While collecting material for *Birds of America*, a project expected to take years, he would also have to find a way to support his wife, Lucy, and their two young sons, Victor and John Woodhouse Audubon. As Audubon's enterprise unfolded, Lucy helped to feed the family, often as the major breadwinner, by teaching. Audubon supplemented the household budget by selling portraits, and he also offered his services as a tutor, which brought him to Oakley House.

His job at Oakley House was to instruct Eliza Pirrie, the fifteen-year-old daughter of Lucretia and James Pirrie. He would be paid sixty dollars a month, along with room and board. In 1821, the annual per capita Gross Domestic Product, a rough indicator of average annual income, was just seventy-three dollars, "so Audubon was very well paid," says economic historian Samuel H. Williamson. According to his arrangement with the Pirries, Audubon could spend half his time instructing Eliza in "drawing, music, dancing, arithmetic, and some trifling requirements such as [styling] hair," and half his time combing the plantation's woodland for birds.

Audubon biographer William Souder has described Audubon's brief but eventful Oakley period as "a revelation," and another biographer, Richard Rhodes, has referred to Audubon's Oakley landscape as "a paradise of birds." "His time at Oakley was one of his happiest and certainly one of his most productive for his bird project," writes contemporary bird artist John P. O'Neill. In his 1937 biography, a quaintly effusive chronicle

Eliza Pirrie
*Portrait image courtesy
of Anne B. Klein*

Receipt detailing payment to Audubon for his teaching services at Oakley
Courtesy Audubon State Historic Site archives, photo by Lori Waselchuk

of the bird artist's life, Stanley Clisby Arthur portrays Oakley as Audubon's "bird heaven."

The area around Oakley, writes another Audubon biographer, Shirley Streshinsky, "was as luxuriant in bird life as any Audubon had known; birdcalls filled the magnificent woods of oak and beech and poplar, of magnolia and holly and cypress . . . Audubon's chance meeting with Eliza Pirrie and her mother had the almost magical effect of placing him in perfect position to observe, to study, and to draw species that would one day make up about a quarter of *The Birds of America*."

Revelation, paradise, heaven, magic—such imagery frames Oakley as an epiphanous Eden of discovery, and for Audubon, the wildlife-rich geography of the Felicianas, an idyllic corner of south Louisiana, truly was a garden ripe with ornithological and artistic insights. While his hope of creating *The Birds of America* was little more than a brainstorm when he came to Oakley, the property's encyclopedic array of bird life renewed Audubon's sense of possibility, lent new perspectives on his emerging artistic technique, and strengthened his resolve to press ahead with one of the most arduous undertakings in the annals of American art.

But Audubon's paradise of birds at Oakley was destined to be a paradise lost. As the summer closed, the plantation mistress fired him under circumstances that remain unclear. Had his exit from Oakley been conceived by a novelist, critics might have deemed it overwritten. Dismissed by the Pirries, a clan whose wealth he resented, the financially straddled Audubon left the plantation even more determined to rise through his art as an aristocrat of merit. The departure of the poor but ambitious Audubon from Oakley, which he sniffingly derided as "an abode of unfortunate opulence," seems much like the impoverished Heathcliff's banishment from the self-assured patrician household of *Wuthering Heights*, Emily Brontë's celebrated 1847 novel.

Like Brontë's brooding anti-hero, who would eventually avenge the indignity of exile by becoming a spectacular success, Audubon used Oakley as a springboard to his destiny as an internationally renowned naturalist and artist. And just as the vindicated Heathcliff reclaimed the very

The Audubon State Historic Site, located 4½ miles southeast of St. Francisville
Map by David Norwood

ground from which he had been estranged, it is one of history's more interesting ironies that Oakley House is now more widely known not for the Pirries, but as Louisiana's Audubon State Historic Site.

Beyond Oakley, in the Felicianas in particular and in Louisiana in general, Audubon endures as a civic and cultural icon, the inspiration for the Audubon Pilgrimage, an annual tour of plantation homes, and the yearly Louisiana Bird Festival. Some forty miles to the south, Audubon commands a continued presence at Louisiana State University's Hill Memorial Library, home to a substantial collection of Audubon prints. In the offices of Louisiana's doctors, dentists, and lawyers, and in the homes of those who can afford expensive good taste, at least one Audubon bird print often hangs on the wall as a small shrine to the man many regard as the founding father of Louisiana's naturalist tradition.

Audubon's abiding influence on Louisiana's contemporary cultural scene suggests that in the broader sense, he never left Oakley, nor did Oakley leave him. The lessons he learned there would help shape an artistic enterprise that would become, in its breathtaking scale and intricate splendor, the Sistine Chapel of American ornithology. Yet the Audubon we meet at Oakley is not the painter savant hovering above us from the grand remove of antiquity. His central preoccupations, the mystery of ecology and the relationship between science and art, give his voice the fresh immediacy of the Internet chat room or morning headline. That might partly explain why the Audubon evoked at Oakley can seem more man than ghost.

Of course, stewards of historical sites typically work hard to create the illusion of the past living in the present. The battlefield, castle, or mansion stands meticulously maintained in a kind of frozen glamour, with artifacts artfully arranged, like stage props in a period drama, to give us selected scenes from the pageant of days long gone. Yet Audubon's durable hold on Oakley seems to transcend tourism's customary promise of history brought to life. His continuing resonance here also issues, one gathers, from the special culture of the Felicianas, an area of Louisiana where the distance between present and past can collapse as casually as the hand fans fluttered by tour guides in plantation homes.

This is the heart of plantation country, after all, where white-columned houses of the Old South decorate the countryside, and where the names etched on nineteenth-century gravestones can seem as vivid in local conversation as the ones in the kitchen phone book. Though Audubon's final resting place lies in New York's Trinity Cemetery, Oakley's neighbors still talk of him as a member of the family. If those who live in and around Oakley House often feel a special claim on Audubon, perhaps it's because Audubon seemed to claim them first. Audubon often publicly identified himself as a Louisiana native son. At one point, he claimed to have been born on a plantation in Mandeville, near New Orleans. This was, as subsequent biographers have learned, one of several stories that Audubon contrived to mask his illegitimacy. In truth, Audubon was born on April 26, 1785, in Saint-Domingue, in what is now Haiti. He was the product of a union between his father, a French sea captain named Jean Audubon, and a twenty-seven-year-old French chambermaid, Jeanne Rabin, who died shortly after Audubon was born.

Audubon spent most of his childhood in France, where he was welcomed and adopted by his father's wife, Anne Moynet. Both Audubon and his family took pains to keep the circumstances of his birth a secret because of the social and legal implications of illegitimacy. By 1803, Audubon was bound for America to escape conscription into Napoleon's army, dispatched by his father to manage Mill Grove, Jean Audubon's farm near Norristown, Pennsylvania. In a provident historical coincidence, Audubon would arrive in the United States the same year that the Louisiana Purchase dramatically expanded the nation's frontier—and the universe of subjects more readily available to Audubon's bird art, an interest he had cultivated since early boyhood.

Mill Grove's neighbors included the young Lucy Bakewell, who became Audubon's wife in 1808. In 1810, the Audubons settled in Henderson, Kentucky, where they established the trading firm of Audubon & Bakewell with Lucy's brother. On July 3, 1812, Audubon became an American citizen, evidence of his optimism about a long future in his adopted country.

Audubon's optimism seemed warranted, given the family's growing prosperity. By the next year, the Audubons had a spacious log cabin in Henderson with four acres of land for his lively menagerie of poultry, livestock, wild birds, and pet rodents—a testament to Audubon's sustained interest in birds and animals. In 1816, Audubon and a couple of business partners invested in the construction of a steam-powered gristmill in Henderson. But by 1819, the mill and Audubon's other businesses would fail, along with those of many others, in a national economic downturn. In his 2004 biography of Audubon, Rhodes points to an intriguing irony: The U.S. economic reverse was at least partially caused by the young American government's debt incurred from the Louisiana Purchase, the very territory that would become the naturalist Audubon's living laboratory. Glimpse Audubon's life in 1819, as he was jailed for unpaid debts and forced to declare bankruptcy, and the lands of the Louisiana Purchase can seem like the mythical sirens who beckoned with their beauty even as they dashed the ambitions of unwary souls.

AUDUBON AS OAKLEY'S MAN AND MYTH

Epic mythology, indeed, might present the only yardstick large enough to measure the profound crisis Audubon faced in 1819—and the subsequent odyssey in which he would, like every sojourner of the world's oldest stories, emerge from his travels a changed man. Destitute, Audubon headed for Cincinnati in 1820, living by his wits as a portrait artist and drawing instructor while his idea for *The Birds of America* slowly coalesced. Since no compendium of American birds would be complete without a survey of the wildlife-rich Mississippi River corridor, Audubon charted an itinerary that, as he initially planned it, would take him down to Louisiana and then into Florida and up the East Coast, gathering specimens and drawing all the way.

Napoleon Bonaparte, whom Audubon idolized, once observed that an army moves on its stomach. Audubon also recognized that his far-reaching ornithological campaign required him to go where he could earn his supper, a reality that brought him to New Orleans in January 1821. The Crescent City, a great center of regional commerce, suggested a promising source of income from portraits and drawing lessons, along with easy proximity to at least some of the birds Audubon intended to include in his volume. But Audubon's artistic scheme was necessarily migratory, and he didn't anticipate staying in New Orleans for long. Even so, his inclination to leave was no doubt strengthened by the city's failure to provide him a steady income.

His work as a drawing instructor had brought him into the fold of the Pirrie family, which divided its time between New Orleans and Oakley. After hiring Audubon to teach Eliza during the Pirries' stay in New Orleans, Lucretia invited him to accompany the family back to Oakley to tutor Eliza until the following winter. The deal also included room and board for Joseph Mason, a young assistant who drew many of the backgrounds for Audubon's bird portraits.

As Audubon related the development in a letter to his wife Lucy, he had charmed Lucretia Pirrie with his versatility as a flutist and singer—gifts which suggested Audubon's competence not only as a drawing instructor to Eliza, but as a general tutor in the finer arts. While there's no reason to doubt Audubon's account of his arrangement with the Pirries, his self-flattering recollection of events poses but one example of his flair for personal promotion, a talent that often skirted—and sometimes crossed—the line between fact and fiction.

Beyond masking the circumstances of his birth, Audubon was not above other exercises in embellishment. He falsely claimed, for example, that his father had been an admiral and his mother a plantation mistress. Audubon also said he had studied under the great artist Jacques-Louis David, an assertion that had no basis in fact. And he recounted hunting with frontiersman Daniel Boone, an incident that never happened. The Boone story was one of many exaggerations Audubon included in his *Ornithological Biography*, a multivolume work that he would sell to subscribers in his post-Oakley years.

"As he had done his whole adult life, Audubon carefully calculated his audience and what it wanted to believe, then blended fact, exaggeration and outright lies into a mélange of self-promotion," Souder writes in his 2004 Audubon biography, *Under a Wild Sky.* "He seemed to take for granted that his subscribers, hungry for tales of derring-do, would accept a larger-than-life version of his experiences in the New World, so that's what he gave them."

In framing Audubon's personal mythmaking as a shrewd attempt at commercial appeal, Souder invites us to consider the intersection between personality and commerce—and how Audubon's blending of the two created one of America's first international celebrities. For what is celebrity, after all, but the magnification of self into a market commodity? In 1830, the same year he was invited to dine with President Andrew Jackson at the White House, Audubon was elected a Fellow of the Royal Society of London, joining the late Benjamin Franklin as the only other

American, at that point, who had been so honored. Those were surely eventful footsteps to follow for Audubon, who had years earlier looked to the rags-to-riches story of Franklin's autobiography for inspiration. Before Audubon, Franklin had charmed the courts of Paris by donning a fur cap and striking the pose of the pioneer philosopher. Audubon followed a similar model when, soliciting the ruling class of England to support his *Birds of America,* he created a sensation by wearing the rough-and-tumble garb of a frontiersman.

Like Franklin, who used eccentric fashion statements, emerging media technology, and the wiles of the raconteur to become a celebrated bon vivant on both sides of the Atlantic, Audubon harnessed publicity and personal flair to cultivate an image that anticipated the modern media star. In another development that portended the present-day environment of media management, Audubon, like Franklin, created a fame that was truly global in scope.

During a century when many seldom traveled farther than a few miles from their birthplace, Audubon's chronology reads like a steamer trunk stamped through a whirlwind of destinations. Born in Saint-Domingue, he would live in France, Pennsylvania, Kentucky, Ohio, Louisiana, England, and New York, among other places, while visiting scores of others.

All of which begs the question: Can Oakley or any single place assert a strong bond with a figure who, in the first half of the nineteenth century, seemed to be everywhere at once? St. Francisville resident Al Troy has compared Audubon's ubiquity with that of Jean Lafitte, a nineteenth-century pirate whose legend looms so large in south Louisiana that folklorists from every hamlet casually proclaim, "Jean Lafitte was here," even when his link to the local geography might be tenuous at best.

This mingling of hyperbole and history, while certainly not exclusive to the South, has played a special role in the regional culture, so long known for its narrative color, its embrace of eccentricity, and its marriage of myth and reality. Those qualities, so central to Audubon's art and writing, identify him to many of those who visit Oakley House as a native son—a man who, while he wasn't born in the area, certainly seemed as if he could have been.

More than a century after Audubon's death, Robert Penn Warren, another genius whose Louisiana period would strongly shape his career, affirmed Audubon as a touchstone of southern letters in "Audubon: A Vision," a 1957 poem cycle in which the title character becomes a point of reference for reflecting on the twin preoccupations of southern literary tradition, land and story. Not surprisingly, Warren's poetic musings on Audubon lead to Oakley House. In a passage that parts the curtain on Audubon's sometimes-troubled time at Oakley House, Warren writes of his hero that "in rich houses, he sat, and knew insult. / In the lobbies and couloirs of greatness he dangled, / And was not unacquainted with contumely."

"THE HAWK THAT POISES IN THE AIR"

Warren also found in his muse, Audubon, a kindred curiosity about the ultimate subject of all creative minds, the cosmic divide between life and death. His consideration of the bird artist eventually brings the reader to Audubon's deathbed, where Warren contemplates the power of art to transcend human mortality. Audubon's alertness to the ephemeral nature of earthly existence—an awareness central to both his pictures and his prose—also resonates with particular power within the southern cultural imagination, which has defined itself over the generations as a running elegy for the passing of time . . . and life itself.

As if to make the point, one of the more memorable passages from Audubon's journal of his Oakley period involves his summons, in the dead of night, to the bed of a dying neighbor. The story unfolds in Audubon's August 1, 1821, journal entry. With its frequent abbreviations—he refers to Lucretia Pirrie, for example, as "Mrs. P"—Audubon's prose also conveys the telegrammatic urgency of a mind on which little was lost:

> We were awakened last night by a servant desiring that I should
> rise & dress to accompany Mrs. P. to a dying neighbor's house,
> about one mile,—We went, but arrived rather late, for Mr. James

O'Connor was dead. I had the displeasure of keeping his body's company the remainder of the night. On such occasions, time flies very slow indeed, so much so that it looked as if it stood still like the hawk that poises in the air over its prey . . . the poor man had drunk himself literally to an everlasting sleep; peace to his soul . . . I made a good sketch of his head and left the house and the ladies engaged at preparing the ceremonial dinner.

Errands of mercy to the Pirries' dying neighbors were not, one can imagine, part of Audubon's original agreement to teach at Oakley. John R. House III, who manages Oakley House as part of the Audubon State Historic Site, points to the incident as a possible indication of Audubon's intimacy with the household. Perhaps Audubon's bond with the Pirries had grown so strong that they felt at ease in enlisting him for the somber vigil for a mortally ill neighbor. But it is also possible, if not likely, that Audubon's deathbed sketch of the Pirries' neighbor was not a spontaneous expression of a tragic moment. Lucretia Pirrie might have known of Audubon's reputation as a master deathbed artist and asked him to go to the ailing neighbor's house for that reason.

In an age when death often arrived without notice and photography was nonexistent, those who could afford such mementoes sometimes commissioned deathbed portraits as a final remembrance of the departed. Two years before his Oakley period, as he was struggling to emerge from bankruptcy, Audubon had made a name for himself as a painter of deathbed portraits in chalk—his renown in this macabre sideline so high, as he recounted it, "that a clergyman residing at Louisville had his dead child disinterred" for an Audubon portrait.

Audubon's skill at drawing the dead so expressively was a natural extension of the methods he had pioneered for his bird portraits. To create his scrupulously executed bird pictures, Audubon was usually compelled to kill his subjects with a gun, mutilating their appearance as little as possible so that the corpses would yield adequate specimens for extended study. Audubon's methods would prompt Warren to observe, in a bit of overstatement, that "Audubon was the greatest slayer of birds that ever lived: he destroyed beauty in order to create beauty and whet his under-standing." In a landmark innovation, Audubon devised a series of stiff wires that could be moved on a board to support his dead bird specimens in poses that persuasively conveyed lifelike attitudes of feeding, flying, or courtship. Audubon succeeded so well at this sleight of hand that modern viewers are often shocked—and sometimes profoundly disappointed—to learn that America's premier naturalist was also a bird killer.

But as some of Audubon's biographers have pointed out, his shooting of the birds he painted was usually a technical necessity. When it was possible, Audubon welcomed the opportunity to work with live speci-mens—a truth borne out by his great pleasure, while at Oakley, in being able to capture and draw a living red-cockaded woodpecker. Even today, ornithologists committed to bird preservation still find it necessary to use a small number of dead birds to advance scientific knowledge. Less than an hour's drive from Oakley House, the LSU Museum of Natural Science boasts one of the world's largest libraries of bird skins—pains-takingly preserved bodies of tens of thousands of birds from around the globe. In long drawers of metal cabinets, tanagers, sparrows, and hawks lie in lively repose. This vibrantly colored morgue, where birds as varied as the macaw and the mockingbird stare blankly from eyes stuffed with cotton, is a valuable resource for artists and scientists who need detailed plumage, morphological, and genetic data about bird species. Despite ornithology's dramatically improved technical capabilities, some birds still lose their lives to help resolve mysteries about their species—and provide critical information for conservation of their populations. Since natural mortality rates in bird populations mean that literally billions die every year, ornithologists know that the mortality they cause is minute, according to ornithologist Van Remsen.

Clearly, Audubon wasn't the first person to kill birds in order to study them, and he wouldn't be the last, though the scale of his bird hunts has raised eyebrows. Even Audubon's admirers have criticized him for oc-casions when he killed far more birds than he could either eat or draw. "Granted, a scientist needs specimens," Audubon scholar Christoph Irm-scher has observed. "But did Audubon really have to obtain birds by, literally, the basketful?" Historical revisionism often resorts to caricature, painting period heroes in grotesque reversals of their popular, pious reputations. Thus Audubon, revered so long and so cloyingly as a frontier Francis of Assisi, can now be too easily dismissed as ornithology's graveyard ghoul. Yet Audubon remains a compelling figure precisely because he was neither angel nor demon, but a mortal genius touched by deep contradictions. The Audubon portrayed in his journals and other writings, as Irmscher has noted, is both "the protector and slayer of birds, irascible, passionate and pugnacious as well as tender, considerate and caring, impressive as well as flawed, attractive as well as repulsive, approachable and then again elusive, like the birds he writes about and to which he would, only half in jest, occasionally compare himself."

Audubon's trying night at the deathbed of an Oakley neighbor, an interlude that alternated between dread and draftsmanlike attention to the details of mortality, offers another bridge between contrasts, revealing a deeply human artist using his gifts of perception to comprehend death and, by extension, to comprehend life. In an eloquent analysis of Audubon's artistic origins, Rhodes suggests that Audubon's early loss of his mother, along with other traumas such as his childhood in the shadow of the French Revolution, influenced his desire to make art that revivified what death too often claimed. But if Audubon masterfully succeeded at rendering his lifeless specimens into incredibly dynamic creatures, it also seems true that his bird pictures, for all their vitality and opulent color, can convey loss as well as life. As Irmscher has mentioned, "many of Audubon's compositions, in spite of their insistent commitment to the recreation of life out of death, are very often dominated by the experience of death, or at least impending death." The swallow-tailed hawk he drew at Oakley—a sleek, black-and-white bird of prey grasping a green garter snake—has the heroism of a hieroglyph, evoking an ancient, vanquished world far removed from our own.

As swampland around Oakley was cleared in subsequent generations, the swallow-tail lost crucial habitat. "Absent for a long period in the parish, the bird has only recently been noted in the past few years in very small numbers in spring," said Keith Ouchley, director of The Nature Conservancy in Louisiana. The swallow-tail's fate would perhaps not surprise Audubon, who occasionally reflected, in his later years, on the effect that human practices were having on bird populations. In a much-quoted journal passage from 1828, Audubon notes that as "time flies, nature loses its primitiveness . . . pictures drawn in ten, or twenty, or more years, will no longer illustrate our delightful America pure from the hands of its Creator!"

"It has been suggested that Warren felt an affinity with Audubon, whose sense of the land and its exploitation was scarcely less agrarian than his own and that of his friends a hundred years later," writes Warren's biographer, Joseph Blotner. Warren's friend and literary contemporary, Eudora Welty, who had inspired his Audubon poem cycle by writing a short story about Audubon called "A Still Moment," once spoke of the artistic ideal in which "the transitory more and more becomes one with the beautiful." We see the fulfillment of that sublime principle in Audubon's bird art. Audubon's personal losses perhaps strengthened his feeling that the larger world, including its natural abundance, was also subject to the sometimes cruel and capricious currents of change.

Of course, Audubon's early and distressingly frequent encounters with death were far from uncommon in his place and time. His was an age of modest life expectancy and high infant and childhood mortality. In the year before he arrived at Oakley, Audubon's seven-month-old daughter Rose had died. Audubon had lost another daughter, Lucy, in 1817. Mason, Audubon's assistant, was also shadowed by grief during his stay at Oakley. Just a month before arriving, he had received news of his father's death.

THE PIRRIES OF OAKLEY

If survivor support groups had existed in 1821, then John James Audubon and Lucretia Pirrie might have found themselves at the same self-help meeting. When visitors to Oakley House ascend the plantation's creaking inner staircase and see the solemn portrait of Lucretia in the manor's morning room, they view a stout, intent woman dressed in black.

Lucretia Pirrie had lost five children by the time Audubon visited in 1821. Women of the period were expected to wear black for up to three years after a death in the family. *Portrait image courtesy of Anne B. Klein*

She spent much of her life in grief. Like Audubon, Lucretia had lost her mother at a young age, and she endured a painful extended separation from her father. In 1781, when Lucretia was eleven, her mother died during an insurrection against the Spanish in Natchez, Mississippi. Her father, who had led the unsuccessful revolt, was captured and sent to a military prison in Cuba, where he stayed for five years. He was released after swearing an oath never to take up arms against the Spanish again.

During her father's absence, the young Lucretia went to live at a convent in New Orleans, where the Ursuline sisters ran a girls' school that taught a variety of subjects, including apothecary. In the room bearing Lucretia's portrait, which still contains Lucretia's medical case of powdered potions, she treated slaves and family members. A door in the corner leads to the exterior staircase that slaves used to enter the room for

The apothecary implements used by Lucretia Pirrie at Oakley House
Photo by Lori Waselchuk

treatment. Since sick call was in the morning, the room became known as the morning room. But it might well have been called the mourning room, defined as it was by the presence of a woman who had lost so much. Oakley House itself originated during a tragic year for Lucretia. In 1799, Lucretia and her first husband, Ruffin Gray, had their slaves begin construction of Oakley House, but before the year was out, Ruffin had died of an unknown illness.

Three years earlier, the Grays, who were living in Mississippi, had received a Spanish land grant of roughly six hundred acres to move to St. Francisville, along with their four children and about twenty slaves, to start a cotton plantation. When Ruffin died, Lucretia petitioned the Spanish crown to allow her to take legal possession of Oakley and its acreage—an unusual request in a time when most women were not allowed to own land in their own name. In what was perhaps a measure of Lucretia's firm bargaining style—a trait that would not work to Audubon's favor—the crown granted Lucretia's request, and Oakley's farming operations continued.

Lucretia married James Pirrie in 1801, and the Pirries enjoyed a thriving American cotton economy. But death, and the threat of death, shadowed Lucretia's time at Oakley. Five of the six children from her first marriage had died by the time she met Audubon, leading some to speculate that Lucretia's interest in apothecary had been deepened by her desire to find something—anything—to safeguard those dearest to her from harm.

The household's troubled health history would figure prominently in Audubon's eventual rift with Lucretia. Eliza was frequently ill, and her doctor, with Lucretia's apparent blessing, ordered her to bed during the last month of Audubon's stay. Audubon found the convalescence excessive, blaming it on the overprotective urges of a mother who had lost so many children. He was eventually dismissed, and there was a subsequent quarrel about whether Audubon should be paid for those days when Eliza was unavailable for instruction.

Audubon described Lucretia as "generous . . . but giving way for want of understanding at times to the force of her violent passions." Such anger, if it indeed unfolded as Audubon described it, would seem an understandable reaction from a woman in Lucretia's situation during the summer of 1821. With her first husband and five children in the grave and another daughter sick with fever, this woman who had also lost her mother so early might well have felt under siege.

Had Eliza not fallen ill, one wonders if Audubon and Lucretia would have been able to develop an enduring friendship. Audubon expressed admiration for Lucretia's industry and declared her "an extraordinary woman." Passages from his journal suggest that the admiration was mutual: "We were called *good* men and now and then received a cheering look from the mistress of the house." The two, indeed, had a potential bond. Each had lost children and parents to the grave, and each—Audubon with his art, Lucretia with her apothecary—used creative talent to answer the threat of mortality.

In James Pirrie, Audubon had an employer who, in many ways, also

James Pirrie
*Portrait image courtesy
of Anne B. Klein*

seemed a kindred spirit. Pirrie's portrait, which hangs above the mantel in the plantation library, flashes the roguish smile of a man who, like Audubon, appeared to have a keen sense of the dramatic. Pirrie, a native of Scotland, had also worked as a millwright, and his business background would have given him much to discuss with Audubon, a former mill owner who had also come from a family grounded in plantation management. Audubon describes Pirrie in his journal as "a man of strong mind but extremely weak of habit and degenerating sometimes into a state of intoxication, remarkable in its kind, never associating with anybody on such occasions and exhibiting all the madman's action whilst under its paroxysm . . . when sober, truly a good man."

Despite Audubon's conclusion that James Pirrie had a drinking problem, the two men seemed to have a genuine rapport. After Audubon and Lucretia Pirrie quarreled about the terms of Audubon's payment, he appealed to James Pirrie to intervene, and James Pirrie did agree to pay Audubon's final bill in full, although Souder writes that the artist never got the money. And after Lucretia Pirrie agreed to let Audubon stay at Oakley a few days past his firing so that he could wrap up some ornithological studies, James Pirrie extended Audubon's stay by yet another night, much to Lucretia's annoyance. If Audubon and James Pirrie enjoyed a bond, it could be that Lucretia's husband suggested to Audubon a sense of the road not taken—what Audubon's life might have been like if his Kentucky businesses had not failed. If not for that reversal of fortune—and Audubon's subsequent commitment to the tenuous life of an artist—he might have become a figure very much like James Pirrie: a prosperous patriarch at the top of the social ladder.

JOHN JAMES AUDUBON SLEPT HERE

It would not have escaped Audubon's attention that his present course, one charted equally by bitter circumstance and vocational choice, had reduced his station and made him a servant to people like the Pirries, not their social equal. This may partly explain his resentment of the Pirries' wealth, and his characterization of Oakley as "an abode of unfortunate opulence."

Audubon's put-down might conjure an image for modern readers of Tara from *Gone with the Wind*, a picture that doesn't adequately convey the real Oakley. In a departure from the iconic antebellum home with imposing round columns and grand rooms, Oakley grew from an earlier and less grandiose architectural tradition.

Instead of a big-columned portico, Oakley has a louvered gallery, a nod to West Indies influences and a practical method for catching much-desired breezes in Louisiana's subtropical climate. When Audubon visited Oakley, the Pirries' homestead and plantations like it were defined by the Regency era, a period inspired by the ancient democracies of Rome and Greece that stressed elegant simplicity, not opulence and ostentation. Oakley's dining room, restored to reflect the tastes of the era, has

Oakley House, part of the Audubon State Historic Site. Audubon entered his bedroom through a door at bottom right.
Photo by Lori Waselchuk

The louvered gallery of Oakley House overlooking Cardinal Trail and the plantation grounds.
Photo by Lori Waselchuk

The winding staircase of Oakley
Photo by Lori Waselchuk

no wallpaper, chandeliers, or velvet upholstery, yet it conveys the kind of tasteful economy popularized by the novels of Jane Austen, who was writing at the time.

The result is a mansion memorable for its sublime understatement, which makes its few architectural flourishes stand out all the more. Perhaps by default, Oakley's most striking physical gesture is the staircase adorning its front. But it is not the staircase, but an unassuming door on Oakley House's first floor, where visitors enter to get their first glimpse of Audubon lore. Here, in a modest brick room, John James Audubon lodged and worked—or at least that is what the historical record suggests.

Audubon's journal records an incident in which he brought a wounded woodpecker back to his room at Oakley to capture its features, the artist toiling away as the bird scaled the room's brick walls, searching for bugs between the cracks. The reference to brick construction locates Audubon's lodgings on the first floor, the only level of Oakley built in brick, and logic suggests this room as the most likely candidate for Audubon's chamber.

The anecdote reminds one that Audubon, with his propensity for bringing wildlife within the walls of polite plantation society, could not have been an easy houseguest. Here's Audubon's account of what happened when he took the bird into his room and attempted to cage it: "He immediately reviewed the premises, hopping about and hunting for a place to work through, and used his chisel bill with great adroitness, sending the small chips he cut to the right & left and having made his way to the floor, ran to the wall and climbed up it as easily as if the bark of his favorite pine had been his foothold, picking between the bricks and swallowing every insect he found . . . remarking often his looking under cracks and the little shelves in the rough wall, I drew him in that position."

Oakley's modern-day caretakers have found remnants of an oven within the bedroom wall, evidence that the chamber had been used as a kitchen in the home's earliest period. Like most plantation owners, the Pirries eventually opted to locate the kitchen in a separate building. The little oven, still visible to those who visit Audubon's bedroom today, recalls an alchemist's laboratory, underscoring Oakley's role as a creative crucible for Audubon's art. There is also something of a monastic quality to the space, which is sparely appointed with a small iron bed, a modest writing desk, and little else.

The room's furnishings, a necessarily speculative recreation of Audubon's period, also include another small bed on a side wall for Joseph Mason. Audubon's young assistant is a muted presence in the Oakley history, and some have charged that this is the way Audubon might have wanted it. Mason drew the backgrounds for many of Audubon's pictures, helping to realize Audubon's innovative concept of depicting birds in their native flora. Before Audubon, birds were usually rendered as isolated images on a white page—lifeless and remote, like so many butterflies pinned on velvet. But Audubon's backgrounds, so meticulously executed by Mason during the Oakley period, give the pictures a breathtakingly persuasive air of documentary reality. In an October 12, 1820, journal entry, Audubon identifies Mason as "about 18 years of age," and various biographers have recorded Mason's age during his Oakley period as either eighteen or thirteen. Even if one accepts Audubon's estimate of eighteen, Mason's depictions of plants show an artist skilled beyond his years.

Mason's handiwork would not, however, be formally recognized in the finished paintings, an omission that offended Mason. But Lois E. Bannon, a scholar of Audubon's art, cautions against reading this as a deliberate slight of Mason. "Audubon biographers who are not familiar with the world of art are often outraged that Audubon did not give credit to his artist assistants in the legend of the prints," Bannon has written in *Audubon: A Retrospective.* "However, until the 20th century, it was not unusual to hire other artists to work on a painting and not acknowledge them. The best known example is Peter Paul Rubens, who painted the subject for a portrait while others painted some of the clothing, the room interiors, landscapes, dogs and horses."

A story passed through generations of the Pirrie family identifies a small, white iron bed as the one used by Audubon, though the account is impossible to document. Many visitors to Oakley are struck by the bed's unassuming scale—6 feet, 4 inches in length, and 3 feet wide. Although people were generally smaller back then, the bed wouldn't have afforded much stretching room for a man who, according to Rhodes, was taller than the period average, with a height of 5 feet, 9 inches.

"George Washington slept here."

"Abraham Lincoln slept here."

"John James Audubon slept here."

Why does this comic cliché of the tour guides carry so much emotional resonance, in spite of its flavor of hometown hype? Perhaps we revere the pillows and blankets of the great and the gone because of an intuitive sense that genius finds its true destiny in the dreaming hours between dusk and dawn. Yet the little bed at Oakley linked to its most famous resident does not convey the limitless horizon of nocturnal vision, but the social constraint of the downstairs servant. We cannot know if Audubon ever slept in that little bed, but it plausibly illustrates the self-effacement that the flamboyant artist was forced to endure for the sake of his work.

Ultimately, however, it isn't likely that Audubon looked within the walls of Oakley House for emotional and spiritual sustenance. Instead, he sought solace and fulfillment in the plantation's ecologically varied woodland—which was, after all, the real point of his visit.

"THE COUNTRY ENTIRELY NEW TO US"

Oakley wasn't Audubon's first choice of destination as summer approached in 1821. He wanted to scout out bird specimens in Florida, and joked in his journal that before his arrival at Oakley, he would have preferred that Lucretia had a plantation available in that nearby state. But once Audubon landed at Bayou Sara, the thriving port community that serviced Oakley and the other homes of nearby St. Francisville, he was immediately impressed by the area's natural abundance.

Audubon marveled at a topography that varied so greatly from the New Orleans he had just left. His June 16, 1821, journal entry conveys the joy of discovery:

> The aspect of the country entirely new to us distracted my mind . . . the rich magnolia covered with its odoriferous blossoms, the holly, the beech, the tall yellow poplar, the hilly ground, even the red clay I looked at with amazement . . . such entire change in so short a time appears often supernatural, and surrounded once more by thousands of warblers and thrushes, I enjoyed nature . . .
>
> My eyes soon met hovering over us the long wished for Mississippi kite and swallow-tailed hawk, but our guns were packed, and we could only then anticipate the pleasure of procuring them

shortly—the 5 miles we walked appeared short. We arrived and met Mr. Pirrie at his house. Anxious to know him, I inspected his features . . . we were received kindly.

Audubon also embraced Oakley, one gathers, as a welcome respite from New Orleans, where he had endured a lapse of fortune and numerous misadventures. Disappointed by the number of portrait commissions he had been able to secure, even in a city widely celebrated as the American Paris, Audubon would conclude after subsequent visits that "New Orleans to a man who does not trade in dollars or any other such stuff is a miserable spot."

Audubon's experiences in New Orleans in 1821 border on the burlesque, playing out like a parody of a city known for its libertine sensibility. Shortly after his arrival, Audubon suffered a hangover, had his wallet lifted by a pickpocket, and was scandalized by the city's nonchalance about public sanitation. Audubon's professional losing streak was broken, however, by a figure who seemed sent from central casting for some period version of *Girls Gone Wild*.

For ten days during his initial stay in New Orleans in 1821, Audubon visited an undisclosed location to paint a picture of a mysterious beauty he called the "Fair Incognito," who had requested that Audubon make a nude portrait of her. A journal entry seems to identify the woman as "Mrs. Andre." Audubon related the story in a letter to his wife—a correspondence in which he seems to congratulate himself on his gentlemanly decorum and marital fidelity in the face of temptation. As compensation for his provocative portrait, Audubon received an expensive souvenir gun from his patroness, who composed this inscription: "Do not refuse this gift from a friend who is in your debt; may its goodness equal yours." The shotgun would come in handy as Audubon later scouted the grounds of Oakley for birds.

Despite its frustrations, Audubon's residence in New Orleans would yield other dividends. Before and after his Oakley period, his stints in the city deeply influenced his artistic development. It was here that Audubon refined a variety of techniques for his work, including watercolor, pencil, and gouache, a way of painting with opaque colors ground in water and mixed with gum. Breakthroughs such as these would create the rich textures and layering of color that became Audubon signatures.

If Audubon could be less than flattering in his views of New Orleans, the city hasn't held a grudge, naming its major park and zoo in the artist's honor. Perhaps it is understood that Audubon's reservations about the locale were, at least in part, an expression of his generalized impatience with urban settings. As a naturalist, Audubon felt most at home in the woods. Oakley, which encompassed thousands of acres at its zenith, proved an embarrassment of riches. But it wasn't just the quantity of Oakley's natural habitat, but its unique qualities that presented a lively laboratory to Audubon. The geography of the Felicianas includes a special confluence of hills, hardwood forests, swampland, and pine flatwoods. The diversity of habitat hosted a living library of American ornithology—so many birds, in fact, that Audubon's accounting of what he saw can seem like Noah stocking his ark.

Audubon's most extensive list of Oakley's bird life occurs in a July 4, 1821, journal entry in which he mixes personal observation with interviews of the locals to give an overview of the area's ornithological bounty. His lengthy entry, written in the jotting style of a reporter on deadline, attests to his renewed intellectual and physical energies after arriving at Oakley. The words "very abundant," "plentiful," "very plentiful," "extremely plenty," and "almost constantly in sight" freckle Audubon's entry like a flutter of exclamation marks, as if Audubon is pinching himself at the multitudes of such birds as the wood thrush, mockingbird, red-bellied woodpecker, titmouse, scarlet tanager, hummingbird, and orchard oriole, among others.

"Was deceived one day by one imitating the cry of the loggerhead shrike, and followed it a great distance before I found my mistake," Audubon writes in his passage on the orchard oriole. "It kept on the tops of high trees in the forest, a very unusual circumstance." Whether the oriole in question mimicked a loggerhead shrike as Audubon suggests is open to question. But the late Roger Tory Peterson, echoing an observation made by many others about Audubon, noted that Audubon, for all of his gifts as a visual artist, was not very discerning with bird song. "Judging by his descriptions of bird voices, Audubon had a very poor ear, particularly when describing some of the high-pitched warblers, which he flatly stated had no song," Peterson writes in introducing a 1981 edition of *The Birds of America.* "Obviously, he had been banging away with his fowling piece so much since his youth that his eardrums were as insensitive as those of some modern rock musicians."

AUDUBON'S RIVAL

Audubon's July 4 entry from Oakley also refers to Alexander Wilson, a figure who seemed to hover over Audubon's shoulder during his sojourn at Oakley—and, indeed, during much of Audubon's life. Wilson, also a bird artist, had died eight years earlier, but his legacy haunted Audubon at every turn. A Scottish immigrant, Wilson had, like Audubon, embarked upon a mammoth reference work of American ornithology. Initially, at least, Wilson seemed to have the upper hand in the race for fame, gaining steam while Audubon was still toying with his *Birds of America* concept.

The men's mutual passion inspired a perhaps inevitable sense of rivalry—at least on Audubon's part—and the feeling lingered, though Wilson's untimely death had cut short his *American Ornithology* series. Although the two men are often remembered as competitors for the same crown, Wilson's audacious bird series, which included seven published volumes at the time of his death, actually helped set the stage for Audubon's work.

As Souder points out, Wilson endured financial and personal sacrifices to help advance an independent scientific culture in America, which was still subordinate to the European establishment. Audubon stood to benefit from this intellectual flowering, though he would also face challenges from Wilson partisans who saw Audubon as a usurper of Wilson's legacy. While Audubon wears the laurel of artistic fame today, Wilson survives only as a historical footnote—evidence not only of Wilson's premature passing, but also of Audubon's superior skill.

Wilson would also become connected to Audubon's stay at Oakley through the picture of the Mississippi kite in Audubon's *Birds of America,* an illustration that had its genesis at Oakley. After the picture's publication, many accused Audubon of copying Wilson's image of the kite as one of two birds in Audubon's print. Souder has concluded the bird in question was, indeed, copied from Wilson, and that Audubon's printer, Robert Havell, plagiarized Wilson as an expedient way to fill out the illustration. "Whatever Audubon thought or said about this outright theft when he discovered it is unclear," writes Souder. What is clear is that Audubon didn't need to borrow from Wilson because he lacked talent of his own.

Wilson's bird pictures, deliberate though uninspired, destined him to play Salieri to Audubon's Amadeus—the diligent technician relegated to the shadow of the more intuitive genius. But Audubon's bid for posterity was little more than a dream in the summer of 1821, which perhaps explains his self-conscious score-keeping with the departed Wilson as he hiked the woods of Oakley. As told in his July 4 journal entry, Audubon peers into mockingbirds' nests and notes "the egg represented by Wilson very little like any of the great number I examined." Audubon also counters Wilson's suggestion that a particular species of hummingbird does not sing, adding, "I have many times listened to its low-toned melody with great pleasure and can assure you that if its voice was as sonorous as it is varied and musical, it would be considered as surpassed by few other species."

Comparing Wilson's picture of the orchard oriole with its real-life counterpart at Oakley, Audubon remarks, with what might be regarded as less-than-restrained one-upmanship, that "the figure of Wilson has the bill much too large & long; the figure of the egg is also too large." Audubon strikes a more magnanimous tone in the final journal entry from his Oakley period, when he says that "the great many errors I found in the work of Wilson astonished me . . . I tried to speak of them with care and as seldom as possible, knowing the good wish of that man, the hurry he was in, and the vast many hearsays he depended on."

AN AUDUBON FOURTH

Audubon's July 4 journal entry, which mentions dozens of bird species, makes no comment on the date's significance as an important national holiday. The omission might reflect the peculiar regional politics of the area, which had not long identified itself as a part of the United States when Audubon came to visit. The Felicianas had been under Spanish rule until 1810, when many of the local residents tired of the arrangement, captured the fort at nearby Baton Rouge, and declared the area an independent state, the Republic of West Florida. Some residents were in favor of remaining independent, while others wanted annexation to the United States.

President James Madison resolved the dispute by proclaiming that the United States had always considered West Florida a part of the Louisiana Purchase. In December 1810, under orders from Madison, Governor William C. C. Claiborne of the Orleans Territory took control of the fort at Baton Rouge by force.

During the region's period of Spanish rule, James Pirrie had served as the local alcalde, an official who represented the Spanish crown. The office held considerable influence, essentially combining the powers of mayor and sheriff within a single position.

The region's recent transition from Spanish to U.S. governance might have inspired relative ambivalence among many of the locals about the Fourth of July. Audubon could also seem generally ambivalent about holidays. His life included more than one instance in which he was on the road or in the field when occasions such as New Year's or Christmas rolled around. Yet we know that Audubon was well aware of the Fourth's significance as a national celebration. One of his most memorable stretches of prose involves his fond memory of a lavish outdoor Independence Day feast in Kentucky in 1808.

Audubon might have regarded his Independence Day toiling in Oakley's ornithological vineyards as a necessary price to pay for his personal independence as a creative artist. Only in embracing the peculiar professional demands of his present existence, or so it seemed, could he realize his potential as an American naturalist.

His July 4 entry from Oakley—so sweeping and detailed that it forms the centerpiece of his Oakley journal—would anticipate another landmark Fourth in the nation's naturalist tradition. On July 4, 1845, Henry David Thoreau set up housekeeping at a small cabin on Walden Pond near Concord, Massachusetts, beginning *Walden,* a seminal text of American literature. It seems nothing more than an accident of the calendar that Thoreau began his peculiar artistic enterprise on the nation's birthday. The holiday also appeared far from Audubon's mind when he embarked upon his extensive census of Oakley bird life on July 4, 1821.

Even so, the historical parallel invites us to consider Audubon as part of a larger naturalist ethic influenced by America's growing sense of national identity. What strikes one rather vividly in reading accounts of Audubon's life is how frequently he's identified with special emphasis as an American. That is clear enough in the title of Stanley Clisby Arthur's 1937 volume, *Audubon: An Intimate Life of the American Woodsman.* The theme continues a generation later in Rhodes's 2004 biography, *John James Audubon: The Making of an American.*

Audubon's profile as a standard-bearer of the American experience might seem like indulgent flag waving on the part of his fans, perhaps suggesting an overly narrow interpretation of a figure who was, in many ways, a truly global citizen. But while both Audubon and Thoreau crafted creative legacies of universal appeal, their intellectual awakenings came not from the Old World institutions of the church or the university, but from a North American landscape still boundless enough to promise infinite revelation.

The ecstasy of discovery conveyed in Audubon's Oakley journal—especially his July 4 entry, which bursts with biblical plenitude—can obscure the formidable obstacles Audubon encountered in surveys of the local bird life. In fact, Audubon's account of his season at Oakley can often read like a bracing piece of summer escapism, a tropical idyll on the order of *Robinson Crusoe* or Melville's *Typee*. But here and there, the hardships of nineteenth-century life on a Louisiana plantation prick the pleasantries of Audubon's travelogue. In his entry of August 1, in which he relates his visit to the deathbed of an Oakley neighbor, Audubon notes "the weather sultry, thermometer at 93." He also mentions, with apparent relief, that the thermometer had not yet risen at Oakley that season past 96 degrees—an acknowledgment, perhaps, of the marginally cooler temperatures that made the Felicianas a prime destination for those who could afford to leave New Orleans during the summer.

A few weeks before his arrival at Oakley, in a May 3, 1821, journal entry from New Orleans, Audubon mentions buying fifteen yards of nankeen for summer clothes—a large expenditure, no doubt, for a man so touched by poverty that at one point he and Mason had been forced to subsist largely on bits of cheese. "Weather since Monday morning very disagreeably hot—thermometer at 88–89—and today at 3 o'clock in the shade at 90," he notes in the same journal entry. That Oakley's relief from the New Orleans heat was only a small matter of degree is obvious in Audubon's opening entry from Oakley, when he mentions his arrival on "a hot, sultry day without any accidents."

Summer in Louisiana also brought mosquitoes, and with mosquitoes came yellow fever, an often fatal illness that claimed more than 41,000 people in New Orleans between 1817, the first year that reliable statistics were available, and 1905, the Crescent City's last epidemic, according to research compiled by the New Orleans Public Library. Although the disease was little understood in Audubon's time, latter-day research would reveal that the illness was spread by mosquitoes carrying the disease from one victim to the other through bites.

Audubon concludes his May 3 journal entry from New Orleans with the somber observation, "cases of yellow fever in the city, I was told." The disease spread more rapidly within the confines of a city, which was yet another reason for people of means to leave New Orleans during the summer. Such considerations could not have been far from the mind of Lucretia Pirrie, who had lost so many children to illness and who would see Eliza fall ill at Oakley before the summer closed. Mosquitoes, heat, and the natural adversities of traversing a strange terrain—all of these factors certainly complicated Audubon's ostensibly idyllic time in the woods of Oakley. But Audubon probably avoided the worst heat of the day by getting into the woods early.

We get a glimpse of his work habits in *Audubon in Louisiana,* an overview of the artist's Louisiana period distributed through the Louisiana State Museum in 1966: "During untold hours in the marshes and forests he developed keenness of observation and patience. He became a man of amazing drive and energy, often rising at three in the morning. He could observe and hunt birds all day, return to camp or to his quarters and draw until dark, then write in his copious journals his observations of the day until the candles burned out late at night."

During Audubon's Oakley stay, of course, teaching duties took time away from birding. But quite often, by the time Eliza Pirrie began her studies with Audubon each day, the artist had probably already done a day's worth of fieldwork. Audubon sometimes reconciled his bird project with his tutoring responsibilities by having Eliza join him at his drawing sessions, teaching her artistic technique as he worked on pictures for *The Birds of America.*

The woods of Oakley span one hundred acres today, a fraction of the thousands of acres comprising Oakley at its high point. The reduced size of the grounds requires visitors to take a leap of imagination to understand the ardent athleticism demanded of Audubon during his forays into the forests of Oakley. Today, visitors hoping to walk in Audubon's footsteps at Oakley stroll down Cardinal Trail—a modest path, covering a third of a mile, that carries birders through woods not far from the mansion.

It's fanciful to assume that Audubon did any serious birding in the area now occupied by Cardinal Trail. Site manager House notes that because of the desire for much-needed air circulation through Oakley House, it would have been untypical to have a forest so close to the house during Audubon's period. Also, the Pirries probably wouldn't have built porches that afforded a view of nothing but trees ten feet away. Although no extensive archaeology has been done on the grounds now covered by Cardinal Trail, property close to the house was customarily used for plantation operations. The wooded area now immediately near Oakley House was, in Audubon's time, possibly not woodland at all.

Audubon would find another change in the Oakley landscape if he returned today—the endless stretches of ardesia, an ornamental plant with bright red berries that decorates Cardinal Trail's understory, creating the impression of walking through an elaborate Christmas wreath. The plant was imported into the region from Southeast Asia, and like similar imports, such as the tallow tree and the kudzu vine, it crowds out native flora. Although no one knows exactly when the plant surfaced at Oakley, ardesia doesn't appear in any pictures of the property up to the 1920s. In such an altered environment, it might seem impossible to appreciate Audubon's feelings of excitement in walking Oakley's woods. But like a medieval miracle play, Cardinal Trail uses a small compass of space to invite reflection on a larger and more arduous odyssey.

That perhaps explains why Cardinal Trail continues to attract a regular stream of birders.

BIRD-WATCHING IN AUDUBON'S FOOTSTEPS

Consider a Saturday in April. The year is 2006, but given the close company that past and present keep at Oakley, the day feels as if it could be any April Saturday in any other year. A small group of birders—Cathy and Al Troy, accompanied by Oakley staffer Judy Butler and I—have gathered at 7 a.m. to walk Cardinal Trail and spot a few birds before the morning gets muggy and bright. Volunteer Tracey Banowetz is along as guide, though the Troys, a husband and wife, are such experienced birders that all of us end up learning from them.

Before we enter the trailhead, as we gather for coffee at Oakley's interpretive center, we spot our first bird of the day: an iridescent blue peacock, appropriately named Indigo, who walks the park grounds as Oakley's unofficial mascot. Peacocks have no historical connection with

The view from Cardinal Trail, a nature path near Oakley House
Photo by Lori Waselchuk

Oakley's Audubon period or to the estate's era as a working plantation. Indigo is the last of a colony of peacocks that arrived at Oakley in later years, under circumstances now unclear.

The peacocks became something of a nuisance to visitors, scratching parked cars with typical peacock profligacy, and so Oakley's caretakers allowed the birds to slowly disappear through attrition. Indigo, the sole survivor, has no real link to Audubon, yet it occurs to the casual observer that the old blue peacock, with its inky, eye-dropping beauty, suggests the kind of in-your-face extravagance one might get in an Audubon print brought to life.

As we begin our birding, a red-bellied woodpecker sounds reveille by tapping out its manic Morse code in the distance. "Do you hear that weeping?" says Cathy, craning her ear toward a plaintive cry ahead of us. "It's a great crested flycatcher." Cathy possibly has a better birding ear than Audubon, who could be tone-deaf about such things, although he did find the sound of this particular species memorable. "The squeak or sharp note of the great crested flycatcher is easily distinguished from that of any of the genus, as it transcends all others in shrillness, and is heard mostly in those dark woods where, recluse-like, it seems to delight," Audubon writes.

Like all birders, the Troys have good binoculars, which would have greatly benefited Audubon's fieldwork. The birding party also has at least one copy of the *Peterson Field Guide to Eastern Birds* on hand. Small enough to slip inside a jacket pocket, the slender volume, known simply as *Peterson* in birding shorthand, contains a wealth of information about birds—their habits, calls, and migratory routes—that was not available in Audubon's time.

Shortly into the walk along Cardinal Trail, Al produces a tape recorder, places it on the ground, and begins playing a tape of a screech owl—its eerie, disembodied voice, which Peterson aptly describes as a "mournful whinny," floating into the tree canopy like an aria rising to the rafters. The gesture seems like the perfect way to scare off birds, but Al explains that the opposite is true. The sound tends to draw down birds to the apparent commotion, like motorists who rubberneck at a car wreck. Within no time, a nearby oak thickens with birds, like a cloud darkening with rain. The visitors include titmice and jays, and one jay caws an alert through the trees, announcing himself as Cardinal Trail's version of the village gossip.

Assigning moral foibles to the excited jay merely follows the lead of Audubon, who viewed blue jays as bad characters and was not afraid to say it. "Who could imagine that a form so graceful, arrayed by nature in a garb so resplendent, should harbor so much mischief—that selfishness, duplicity and malice should form the moral accompaniments of so much physical perfection!" he writes. Audubon accuses the jay of any number of crimes, including raiding the nests of other species and annoying farmers. "He is more tyrannical than brave," Audubon says of the jay, "and like most boasters, domineers over the feeble, dreads the strong, and flies even from his equals."

Audubon's antipathy to the blue jay would have placed him in large company around Oakley, where concerns about the bird's consumption of food crops made him a public enemy. "Last April, immense numbers of these birds so annoyed the corn rows in this neighborhood as to force the planters to poison them with corn boiled with arsenic, which had a great effect—killed the thieves often instantly," Audubon ominously reports in his Oakley journal. He also mentions that in his extensive ramblings of Oakley, he encountered not more than a dozen jays—a telling reflection of Oakley's poisoning program, given the jay's typically ubiquitous presence throughout the eastern United States.

One wonders what Audubon would have thought of Al's tape recorder, this curious piece of sorcery in which a bird's music is trapped in a box, then spilled once again into the landscape, tricking titmice and jays into open view. It's an innovation that he would have had great difficulty conceiving, and but one of many ways in which today's birding hobbyist comes better equipped than Audubon.

But while Audubon didn't have many of the standard-issue tools of the modern birder, he boasted at least one advantage that many contemporary birders lack: a remarkably disciplined attention span. Audubon's laserlike focus lies at the center of one of the most colorful anecdotes of his Oakley stay, his encounter with several red-cockaded woodpeckers. We already know that Audubon brought one woodpecker back to his bedroom at Oakley so that he could draw it, a misadventure in which the bird escaped his cage and began rifling the brick crevices of Audubon's chamber for bugs. Equally eventful was the field excursion that preceded that bit of bedroom farce.

Audubon tells the story in his July 29, 1821, journal entry:

> I had the pleasure of meeting with several red-cockaded woodpeckers yesterday during a walk we took to the pine woods, and procured two beautiful males, both alive, being slightly wounded each in the wing—the particular and very remarkable cry of this bird can be heard at a very considerable distance of a still day. In

articulation, it resembles that of the hairy woodpecker, but it is much more shrill & loud. The tall pine trees are its chosen haunts, and seldom does it alight on any other kind of timber—its motions are quick, graceful and easy. It moves in all directions, either on the trunk or limbs, looking often very cunningly under the loose pieces of bark for insects; [it] is more shy than any of its genus. Watching attentively all our movements below, they kept always on the opposite side, peeping carefully at us. The second one shot did not lose a moment to think of its misfortune. The moment it fell to the ground, it hopped briskly to the nearest tree, and would soon have reached its top had I not secured it. It defended itself with courage and so powerfully did it peck at my fingers that I was forced to let him go . . .

Confined to my hat on my head, they remained still and stubborn. I looked at them several times, when I found them trying to hide their heads as if ashamed to have lost their liberty. The report of my gun alarmed them every time I shot, when they both uttered a plaintive cry—Through the pain of the wound or the heat felt in my hat, one died before we reached Mr. Pirrie's house—the other I put in a cage.

The reader's first thought about this passage is that the experience was far from pleasant for the woodpeckers. But then again, it was no picnic for Audubon, either, although the scene, which unfolds like a piece of prime-time situation comedy, does offer a certain amount of grim comic relief. His hand wounded by the formidable aggressions of a woodpecker—a creature designed to chip wood into confetti—Audubon places two of the birds in his hat, which he returns to the top of his head. And then, with his hand no doubt throbbing, and his scalp assaulted by two angry woodpeckers, Audubon nevertheless continues his hunting, an enterprise demanding sustained alertness and sharp aim.

Audubon's ability to carry off such a feat suggests a talent for prolonged attention that borders on Zen-like trance. There is, of course, always the possibility that Audubon's woodpecker story is just another one

Clues from Audubon's journal suggest that he slept in a modest room on the
first floor of Oakley.
Photo by Lori Waselchuk

A small cage in Audubon's
bedroom at Oakley House
represents the artist's occasional
practice of capturing bird
specimens for study.
Photo by Lori Waselchuk

of his tall tales. But to consider the yield of Audubon's career—hundreds of bird pictures, executed with unprecedented detail, in a relatively brief amount of time—is to realize that no artist could have accomplished so much without watching, watching, watching to the exclusion of nearly everything else.

"You could not ask for a worse day for bird-watching," a dejected Cathy says as the birding party returns from Cardinal Trail to the parking lot. On this overcast morning, many of the birds appear in the trees only in silhouette, and Cathy has wished for a bit more sun to back-light the birds, like figures in a studio, so that we can appreciate their plumage.

The otherwise pleasant morning carries a reminder that in birding as in fishing, success depends not only on earnest ambition, but on weather, timing, and luck. It makes all the more impressive the accomplishment of Audubon, a man who could traverse the woods for hours, yet sometimes emerge, like all birders, with little to show for his trouble.

The morning's bird-watching has worked up appetites, and as the Oakley birders file back to their cars, thoughts of lunch are not far behind. After his own birding, Audubon satisfied his hunger back at Oakley's dining room, where journal entries suggest that he ate with the rest of the family.

AN AUDUBON REPAST

Family ledgers that survive from the period indicate that the Pirries were wealthy enough to savor delicacies not available to most householders of the era—quite a change of cuisine for Audubon, who had subsisted only a few days before in New Orleans on cheese, a bit of ham, and salted mackerels. As in many plantation mansions that are now open to the public, Oakley's dining room has the table set with exquisite china and dinnerware, as if perpetually waiting for the next meal to begin. Notably, no one at Oakley claims that Audubon hand-painted the family china while he was there, though other plantations and households throughout the

South have made such a claim about some of their own heirloom china. We do know that Audubon, who loved to discuss his artistic pursuits in scrupulous detail in his journals and letters, never mentioned painting china. "As someone in St. Francisville once commented to us," Audubon investigators Mary Durant and Michael Harwood once wrote, "if Audubon had painted all the dinner plates he is reported to have painted, he wouldn't have had time to do anything else."

The artful arrangement of the place settings in Oakley's dining room reminds us that in the nineteenth century, dinner was a form of theater, with conversation as the principal means of entertainment. It was a forum that uniquely suited Audubon, a man whom House once aptly described as "the nineteenth-century version of television." With his gift for anecdote, his unusual occupation, and his keen sense of the dramatic, Audubon would have been an eventful visitor to Oakley's table, and his news and narratives would have been all the more welcome, perhaps, given Oakley's distance from the city. Today, not far from Oakley's dining room, it's possible to hear the whisper of wheels from nearby Highway 965, a busy tributary of traffic from the interstates that quickly connect the world in a web of immediacy. That makes it hard to imagine the relative isolation of circa 1821 Oakley, which would have stood within the wooded wilderness like a feudal castle.

Like the stone fortresses of medieval Europe, Oakley also hosted its share of important emissaries. Among the visitors to Oakley during Audubon's stay were Louisiana's governor, Thomas Robertson, whom Audubon commended as "a really true philosopher of the age," and John Clay, the brother of nationally known lawmaker Henry Clay.

The guest list at Oakley that summer suggests that there was provocative banter across the dinner table, and there would have been much to talk about. The world of 1821 that summer hummed with possibility. America was a young country during Audubon's season at Oakley. House likes to remind visitors that in 1821, the memory of George Washington and other founding fathers was still fresh. Beethoven was still alive. On May 5, 1821, only weeks before Audubon's arrival, Napoleon Bonaparte, whom Audubon admired, had died in St. Helena. Lord Byron was the literary toast of England, and fellow poet John Keats had just passed away, much too young, that February.

Interestingly, Keats had little use for Audubon because of a soured business deal between Audubon and Keats's brother, George. Closer to home, in Washington, Congress was navigating the final portion of the Missouri Compromise, an agreement, brokered by Henry Clay, that sought to reconcile the country's emerging debate over slavery. That would have been of no small interest to the Pirries, whose wealth was based on slave labor.

John James Audubon—naturalized American, world traveler, man of art and science—seemed particularly suited to the age's boundless intellectual ambition, and Oakley's table presented a promising venue for his opinions. Like any good dining companion, he could also be entertaining. His accounts of birds and animals, so often framed with gladiatorial flare and an eye for dramatic detail, seemed to anticipate the swashbuckling style of TV nature documentary. Were Audubon alive today, he would probably have his own cable show.

But if Audubon inspired attention from others at Oakley's dinner table, it is also likely that he was observing them at least as intently as they were watching him. He was, in addition to being a bird-watcher, a practiced people watcher, too. His journals, which sound themes that would later be elaborated in his other writings, offer more than ornithological field studies. Alert to the quirks of the characters he would meet in his quest to make the great American bird book, Audubon also had a novelist's appreciation of the oddball variety of the human pageant.

Almost all of what we know of the social relationships within Oakley House that summer comes from Audubon's journals. It's a necessarily lopsided narrative, told as it is from Audubon's vigilantly self-justified point of view, but its emphasis on dialogue and character sketch reveals a man who was deeply interested in the mechanics of storytelling.

For whom was Audubon writing these journals? Less than a year before, on November 28, 1820, Audubon passed a rainy morning by entering into his journal a detailed autobiographical sketch directed to his sons. At least one intended audience for Audubon's journal was his immediate family. But the careful posturing within these journals also suggests a man already seeking a broader public stage for his writing.

That stage would come in 1831, with the publication of the first installment of Audubon's multivolume *Ornithological Biography*, a compendium of stories and observations about the birds he'd met in his American explorations. Audubon's editor, William MacGillivray, suggested that Audubon appeal to the general reader by breaking up the many bird studies with a series of essays, "Delineations of American Scenery and Character." While inspired by editorial expedience, MacGillivray's scheme also carried a tacit acknowledgment of Audubon's gifts not only as a visual artist, but as a vivid storyteller.

JOHN JAMES AUDUBON, OAKLEY SCRIBE

"We are all familiar with Audubon the painter," Scott Russell Sanders writes in introducing *Audubon Reader*, a 1986 anthology of Audubon's best prose. "Reproductions of his vivid birds and beasts hang in our courthouses, lie in slick books on our coffee tables, decorate our bedrooms and greeting cards. Say his name, and in the minds of most listeners a colored print will arise. But Audubon was also a writer, and a remarkable one." Sanders's critical assessment has been affirmed in recent years by renewed appreciation of Audubon's writing. The Library of America, which reserves its editions for the country's best writers, gave Audubon the nod in 1999 with the publication of *John James Audubon: Writings and Drawings*. Richard Rhodes followed suit in 2006 with another *Audubon Reader*, an elegant testament to Audubon's enduring literary reputation.

One reason that Audubon is less known as an author than as an artist is his unschooled syntax, which suggests the hurly-burly improvisation of frontier folklore. His texts do not, in short, shimmer with the kind of polished perfection that invites automatic acclaim within the academy.

The prose is so unorthodox, in fact, that many books about Audubon, including this one, change much of his punctuation, spelling, and grammar in the interest of clarity. Audubon had little formal schooling and used English as a second language. As Sanders reminds readers, Audubon also wrote at a time when conventions of spelling were less uniform, so that even learned commentators such as Thomas Jefferson spelled erratically.

A signature element of Audubon's prose is his penchant for capitalization, a habit indulged so freely that one would be hard pressed to discern any method in his madness. Whether he is talking about Warblers or Water, Cypresses or Supper, Indians, Evenings or Eggs, Audubon's jottings announce the everyday in big script. In literature as in life, the flamboyant Audubon refused to be confined to the lower case. His Oakley journals, like so much of his writing, recount capital adventures in capital letters.

Audubon's sentences, with their thickets of tall letters shading every line like some primeval forest, give his texts the flavor of a fairy tale. So the reader is not surprised to learn from Audubon's journals that as he embarked on the voyage that would take him to Louisiana, he carried a copy of a favorite book, the fables of La Fontaine, along for the ride. Jean de La Fontaine (1621–1695) had gained fame by borrowing freely from Aesop's fables and weaving them into witty poems—most of them, like their source material, concerned with the fanciful vanities of animals in human situations. His works would have been among the national classics as Audubon was growing up in France, but Audubon's longstanding affection for La Fontaine's works hints at something more than nodding respect for a French icon.

La Fontaine's influence seems most marked in the anthropomorphism of Audubon's bird subjects, as when Audubon castigates the blue jay for its thievery and other moral failings. But while La Fontaine's fables dress up donkeys, pigeons, storks, and other creatures in human attire, the way a modern pet owner might slip a sweater over a poodle, they ask us to do more than buy into the premise that animals are people, too. The flip side of these animal fables is their implicit invitation for humans to imagine what it might be like to be another creature. For Audubon, such a creative exercise was not only a means of entertainment, but an occupational imperative. Like all successful hunters, his ability to find birds rested in the ability to think like a bird—to essentially become one with his subjects—for hours at a time.

In 1821, vicariously experiencing the life of birds was a particularly romantic enterprise for the great romantic Audubon, who was living in what would become known as the great age of romanticism. Modern aviation was still a distant concept, and the act of flight had not yet been deconstructed into a merely mechanical feat.

Since "the very dawn of civilization, birds were symbols of the spirit," the poet J. D. McClatchy has written. "Falcon or dove, stork or raven or owl, they were our messengers, fierce or gentle intermediaries between our earthbound lives and the upper air. In Egyptian hieroglyphs, Greek myths, Biblical accounts, tribal chants, and popular legend, they were omens and emblems to be longed for or feared. Always and everywhere, with their uncanny freedom and their exquisite song, they were our sense of soul, the premonition and instance of a life beyond our own."

It is a measure of Audubon's gifts as an artist that even in today's age of aviation, in which flight so often becomes a grudging means to an end rather than an exhilarating end in itself, his pictures continue to reconnect us with the wonder and mystery of avian life. Throughout his Oakley ouevre, whether he documents the darting whimsy of the summer tanager or the rapturous color of the indigo bunting, Audubon's images, like the poems of La Fontaine, retain the revelatory power of myth.

To place Audubon within the tradition of mythmaking involves some degree of irony, since he's been accused of slipping the leash of literal truth in the service, not of art, but of tabloid sensationalism. Exhibit A in the case against Audubon's veracity is a striking image, undertaken at Oakley, of several mockingbirds in epic battle against a marauding rattlesnake. The snake has climbed a tree, coiling itself around the trunk in the pursuit of the mockingbirds' eggs, which rest in their nest as enticingly as an entrée on a dinner plate. But a noble mocker, its wings spread like an archangel, clings to the side of the nest in defiant defense, the rattlesnake answering the challenge with fangs as open and sharp as a bear trap.

The picture is mesmerizing and brims with biblical portent, as if Eden itself is falling before our eyes. The apocalyptic drama of the scene, which chills us like an encounter with an Old Testament fresco, seems all the more compelling because Audubon saw it himself.

Or did he?

By necessity, much of Audubon's bird paintings involved dramatic recreation—the careful positioning of dead specimens in lifelike positions meant to simulate natural behavior. In a journal entry of August 25, 1821, Audubon notes the completion of a rattlesnake drawing, and that Eliza had also drawn the same snake. "Anxious to give it such a position as I thought would render it most interesting to naturalists, I put it in that which that reptile generally takes when on point to inflict a most severe wound," he adds. In a passage that underscores some of the more disagreeable challenges of his craft, Audubon also suggests that in the high heat of a Louisiana summer, he and his pupil were in a race against time to document the snake before it decomposed.

But what seems open to debate is whether Audubon's eye-popping portrayal of a rattler raiding a mockingbird's nest was grounded in his field observations. The question would become part of a larger controversy concerning other claims that Audubon made about the rattlesnake's typical habits. In his *Ornithological Biography* entry on mockingbirds, Audubon observes that various "species of snakes ascend to their nests, and generally suck the eggs or swallow the young; but on all such occasions, not only the pair to which the nest belongs, but many other mockingbirds from the vicinity, fly to the spot, attack the reptiles, and, in some cases, are so fortunate as either to force them to retreat, or deprive them of life."

According to the American International Rattlesnake Museum, "rattlesnakes can climb, but rarely do." In a scientific paper delivered during Audubon's stay in Edinburgh and published in 1827, Audubon made more flamboyant claims about rattlesnake behavior. He tells of a snake climbing into the upper branches of a tree to capture and swallow a gray squirrel. And Audubon shares as well authenticated a yarn about a farmer dying of a rattlesnake fang embedded in his boot, followed by the deaths of two sons months later—after they took turns wearing their father's boots.

Audubon's scientific paper on the rattlesnake drew heated criticism from rivals, but the criticism also rallied Audubon's supporters, John Chalmers writes in *Audubon in Edinburgh*. "Audubon was not one to allow strict accuracy to interfere with a good story," Chalmers observes of Audubon's rattlesnake reportage, "and one wonders whether this was not an example of this tendency."

AUDUBON'S OAKLEY HUNTING GROUND

In a 1946 address marking the ninety-fifth anniversary of Audubon's death, scholar Robert Cushman Murphy suggests that Audubon's factually suspect account of rattlesnake behavior might have been driven by professional pressures. "Audubon was presumably cajoled into rather too much writing and publication in 1827," says Murphy, advancing a theory shared by numerous Audubon commentators.

If Audubon were in search of a few quick anecdotes to season a naturalist narrative, he needn't have gone any farther than the rich repository of hunting tales developing along the American frontier. Audubon would have been connected with this community since he was not only an artist of birds, but an accomplished hunter. That's why Oakley's dining room, refurbished by local members of the Daughters of the American Revolution, is such a promising window into Audubon's art. It reminds visitors that in 1821, even in plantation homes stocked with the bounties of kitchen gardens and store-bought culinary delights, hunting was both an outdoor pastime and a regular means of sustenance.

Records of the Oakley household from the 1820s document lavish shipments of salmon, chocolate, almonds, oysters, turkeys, and oranges for the plantation's table. In spite of such choices, the Pirries also supplemented their menu with wild game. "They ate game for the sake of variety," says House.

In a July 22, 1821, journal entry, Audubon mentions that a Native American of the Choctaw tribe who hunted for the Pirries' table has brought him a female specimen of "the chuck will's widow in full and handsome plumage." Audubon would not have found it ironic that the same man supplying game for the Pirries' meals was also providing him potential subjects for paintings. For Audubon, hunting and ornithology were not radically different endeavors, but mutually enriching disciplines. Obviously, the hunter and the bird-watcher rely on a shared set of skills: patience, sharp observation, and an ability to anticipate the behavior of their quarry.

Audubon was an expert hunter who periodically used his skills to feed himself and his family. In an era before stringent game laws, he sometimes killed many birds at one time. Contemporary birders, including many who look to bird-watching as an alternative to blood sport, can find it difficult to square Audubon's artistic exaltation of birds with his hunting life. But Audubon's hunting background is not a negative for all potential admirers, and in Louisiana, where hunting remains a popular pastime, Audubon's skill with a shotgun might be regarded in many circles as a cause for endearment rather than estrangement. Drive north into Oakley country from nearby Baton Rouge, and the roadside shops, with their camouflage gear and skinning knives, remind the traveler that Audubon wasn't the last hunter to visit the Felicianas.

Audubon's command of the manly arts—tracking, marksmanship, and outdoor survival—offers a lively contrast with the modern stereotype of the ornithologist as a dilettante in a pith helmet. When Murphy describes Audubon as a "Dead-Eye Dick with the flintlock, and with the percussion pieces used by sportsmen in his later days," he evokes frontier heroes from boyhood adventure novels. "He was a man's man," says Elisabeth Dart, president of the Friends of Oakley, the plantation's nonprofit support organization. "He could hunt, and he could dance. There was nothing foppish about him, except his temper."

Whatever it adds or subtracts from Audubon's stature among modern observers, his enthusiasm for hunting belongs to a much larger tradition in American naturalism. "Henry David Thoreau, notorious nature lover, was also a hunter and fisherman, on occasion," the great twentieth-century naturalist Edward Abbey once reminded readers. Abbey quotes Thoreau's admission that "if I were to live in a wilderness, I should become . . . a fisher and hunter in earnest." In a probing essay on the ethics of hunting, Abbey makes a crucial distinction between hunting for sustenance and hunting for mere sport. It's a distinction that can be indicting for Audubon, who sometimes, particularly in his early years, killed more birds than he could use for either the table or his art.

"John James Audubon, who can stir the tenderest emotions in any breast when he recreates birds with his brush or his pen, proves to have been a man imbued with a primordial hunting instinct," says Murphy. "In his younger days, at least, he killed tirelessly for sport." The tension of Audubon's inner contradictions is precisely what makes him such an absorbing character, Sanders has observed. "In Audubon's own day, you could have found more accomplished hunters or scientists; in our time you could find more zealous conservationists and finer artists," writes Sanders. "What makes Audubon extraordinary and what charges his writings with inner drama is the *fusing* of these roles, the fierce interplay of identities."

But Murphy, like many Audubon scholars, also notes Audubon's growing sensitivity, as he matured, to the implications of overhunting. As one example of Audubon's deepening grasp of ecology, Murphy points to a March 16, 1821, journal entry from New Orleans—just a few weeks before Audubon's arrival at Oakley. On that eventful March day, Audubon witnesses the passage of "millions of golden plovers" coming from the north—and their widespread slaughter by hundreds of waiting hunters. It leads Audubon to soberly note that "the destruction of these innocent fugitives from a winter storm above us was really astonishing." Audubon estimates that if each of the 400 or so hunters had killed 30 dozen plovers that day—a casualty rate he suggests is quite conservative—"that day 144,000 must have been destroyed." Audubon credits—or blames—the consummate skill of Louisiana hunters for the carnage, observing that "the sportsmen are here more numerous and at the same time more expert at shooting on the wing than anywhere in the [United] States."

Audubon's calculation, if correct, suggests that for all its deadly efficiency, the body count from that day's plover hunt represented a tiny fraction of the birds that had moved across the New Orleans sky like a front of dark weather. Audubon's surprise at the scale of the plover shoot didn't dissuade him from raising his own gun in the search for specimens. In Audubon's time, wildlife was so fantastically plentiful that it was difficult for many Americans to fathom the need for conservation policies such as bag limits and state-specified hunting seasons. For that reason alone, it's equally difficult to judge nineteenth-century figures such as Audubon by today's standards of ecological enlightenment.

Not everyone, however, excuses Audubon's excesses as a mere period pathology. "Apologists for Audubon's industrial-style killings have pointed out that he 'was a man of his time,' ignoring the fact that even in those days 'in which marksmanship with living targets was an admired sport in itself' there were some dissenting voices," Irmscher writes. "The first laws for the protection of game were introduced at the time that Audubon was working on the octavo edition of *The Birds of America*. An early New York law of 1838, later repealed, prohibited the use of multiple guns in the killing of waterfowl; in 1844, the New York Association for the Protection of Game was established; a few years later Rhode Island outlawed the spring shooting of wood duck, black duck, woodcock, and snipe."

Chalmers suggests that while some of Audubon's contemporaries were answering environmental storm clouds with plans of action, "Audubon, too, recognized the adverse impact of man on the environment but did less about it in practical terms." "Audubon's real contribution was not the conservation ethic but awareness," Peterson once wrote. "That in itself is enough; awareness inevitably leads to concern." As a man who was watching the transformation of the American landscape, a shift that was unfolding as he experienced dramatic swings in his personal fortunes,

Audubon knew that change was life's only constant. Even so, he seemed surprised—and deeply wounded—when Lucretia Pirrie fired him as Eliza's tutor.

A PAINED FAREWELL

No one can say, with any degree of certainty, why Lucretia Pirrie fired Audubon in October 1821. The only account of the dismissal comes from Audubon himself, who pleads his case in an October 20, 1821, journal entry that recounts his deteriorating relationship with the Pirrie family and his firing several days earlier. Three months out of the four that he and Joseph Mason spent at Oakley "were spent in peaceable tranquility," says Audubon. "Seldom troublesome of disposition, and not caring for or scarcely ever partaking of or mixing with the constant transient visitors at the house, we were called *good* men and now & then received a cheering look from the mistress of the house, and sometimes, also, one glance of approbation of the more circumspect Miss Eliza." Audubon's suggestion that he didn't care to mix with Oakley's visitors seems to slightly contradict his flattering accounts of meeting the governor of Louisiana, John Robinson, as well as John Clay at Oakley.

During the last month of Audubon's stay at Oakley, Eliza Pirrie became seriously ill. Eliza's sixteenth birthday fell on October 5, and she probably spent it in bed, her prognosis uncertain. Audubon doesn't mention Eliza's birthday—a telling indication, perhaps, of his growing detachment from the family. But the irony of a young girl's birthday darkened by illness would not have been lost on Lucretia Pirrie, who had already lost five children in just a few years. Because of these losses, notes Audubon, there was a lot of concern in the household about Eliza's survival. "No doubt much too much care was taken of her; kept in bed long after she was convalescent and not permitted to leave her room for a long time, she became low of flesh and crabbed of speech." Eliza's doctor, whom Audubon mockingly describes as "the *man she loved,*" limited Audubon's access to Eliza and, according to Audubon, told Lucretia that it would be best for Eliza's recovery if she didn't draw, write, or otherwise pursue her studies for some months. Since Audubon was supposed to stay at Oakley only through the winter, this diagnosis alone, if Lucretia took it to heart, would have made Audubon's continued employment beside the point.

"I saw her during this illness at appointed hours as if I was an extraordinary ambassador to some distant court—had to keep the utmost decorum of manners, and I believe never laughed once with her the whole 4 months I was there," Audubon writes. Eliza's doctor did, however, encourage her to eat as much as she pleased, and Audubon remarks, again with sarcasm, that Eliza followed this prescription with unreserved enthusiasm.

Although popular history often explains Audubon's firing at Oakley as a disagreement about money, this seems a misreading of Audubon's journal. Audubon and Lucretia did, indeed, argue about the terms of his final payment, but this dispute appears to have surfaced after Lucretia had already fired Audubon. Audubon doesn't mention the argument until some paragraphs after his news of the firing, and it doesn't seem to be the cause of his dismissal. Audubon and Lucretia quarreled because in his final bill, he charged for fifteen days of instructional time during which Eliza had been ill. Audubon thought his bill was well within the spirit of his original agreement with the Pirries, but Lucretia accused him of cheating and refused to pay Audubon on his terms.

Audubon sent the bill to James Pirrie, noting that Lucretia's husband "was then laboring under one of his unfortunate fits of intoxication." As Audubon tells it, James Pirrie later came to see him, apologized for Lucretia's behavior, and directed his son-in-law, Jedediah Smith, to pay Audubon's bill.

While Audubon seems to have gotten along fairly well with the men of the Oakley household, his relationship with the Oakley women was strained. Jedediah and his wife, Mary Ann, Lucretia's daughter by her first marriage, were staying at Oakley at the time. As Audubon notes in his journal, he and Mary Ann did not get along. Audubon accuses Mary Ann of directing "the grossest words of insult" at both him and a portrait of Lucretia that he was finishing up on behalf of Eliza, who had started the picture. "She bursted at another time in a ridiculous laugh at table," Audubon writes of Mary Ann, "when her good husband interfered and told her she ought to make me some amends for her conduct—I left the table unwilling to hear any more of this."

Oakley House, though spacious, wasn't large enough to easily accommodate such clashes of personality. And in any contest between Mary Ann Smith and Audubon, there's little doubt about whom Lucretia would have supported. Although it might not have been the principal cause of Audubon's departure, his unpopularity with Mary Ann couldn't have helped.

One of the more colorful—and perhaps least supportable—theories concerning Audubon's dismissal is the notion that he was fired because of a scandalous romantic interest in Eliza. Drawing on local lore that is difficult to document, Alice Ford popularized this theory in her 1964 biography, *John James Audubon*. "Toward summer's end the servants and house guests and even the neighbors began to spread talk about Eliza's rapport with her thirty-six-year-old drawing master," writes Ford.

Souder touches on the theme in his 2004 biography. While he stops short of directly linking Audubon's dismissal with a sexual issue, he mentions that Audubon "took note—perhaps not appropriately—of the 'good form'" of Eliza's body. Audubon did offer a physical description of Eliza in a passage from his journal recalling his firing: "Miss P. had no particular admirers of her beauties, but several very anxious of her fortunes, amongst which a certain Mr. Colt, a young lawyer who appeared quite pressing, although very uncivilly received at times." In a subsequent paragraph, Audubon says: "This daughter Eliza of age 15 years, of a good form of *body*, not handsome of face, proud of her wealth and of herself, cannot be too much fed on praise—and God knows how hard I tried to please her in vain—and God knows also that I have vowed never to try as much again for any pupil of mine—as usual I had to do 2/3 of all *her* work. Of course, her progresses were rapid to the eyes of everybody, and truly astonishing to the eyes of some good observers."

Much of Audubon's concern about Eliza's appearance seems connected to her suitability as a bride, the primary role for women in Audubon's time. Women in Eliza's day and age often married when quite young. In that context, Audubon doesn't seem particularly unseemly in remarking on Eliza's marital prospects—especially when, as Audubon notes, her presence in a prominent plantation family would have attracted suitors.

As an artist, Audubon was frequently alert to physical appearance, and his stated observations on the subject cannot be taken as automatic proof of sexual interest. At his very first meeting with James Pirrie, for example, Audubon records that "anxious to know him, I inspected his features." The legend of an Audubon-Eliza dalliance might also be grounded in the idea of Audubon as a French romantic. "He *was* a flirt," Streshinsky writes of Audubon. "He gave freely of his kisses and reveled in female company, peppering instructions to his pupils with 'my darling' and 'my sweet girl.' But it is unlikely that he was anything more than his usual charming self with Eliza, or that she responded to him. For one thing, against her mother's wishes she had already set her cap for her cousin Robert Barrow, with whom she was to elope within a year."

Just before his arrival at Oakley, Audubon's journal records his dismissal by Dr. Louis Heerman of New Orleans, who had hired Audubon to teach drawing lessons to his wife. Heerman's wife had accused Audubon of making advances toward her, which Audubon saw as revenge for her unreciprocated advances toward him.

Audubon's New Orleans interlude with his nude painting subject, the "Fair Incognito," would also advance his reputation for subsequent generations as a libertine. But Audubon shared a detailed account of his sessions with the "Fair Incognito" with his wife as an apparent testimonial to his marital fidelity, even under the strain of numerous temptations and long periods of separation. Irmscher has suggested that Audubon's "Incognito" story, which came at a time when his wife, Lucy, was growing impatient with his bird project, might have been "deftly doctored to stir up his wife's jealousy, a testosterone-powered potboiler with generous references to female nudity. Or so it seems." Whatever the motivations behind the "Fair Incognito" letter, an intense and detailed correspondence between Audubon and Lucy suggests a passionate marriage unblemished by infidelity. "To judge from the abundant, detailed, and extremely frank and intimate records of his journals and letters, he was devoted wholly and completely to Lucy Bakewell from the moment he fell in love with her until the end of his life," writes Murphy.

Whatever Audubon felt about Eliza, his stance toward her was never neutral. His opinions regarding Eliza were strong, but all over the map. In his August 25, 1821, journal entry, he refers to "my amiable pupil, Miss Eliza Pirrie," and says, "it is with much pleasure that I now mention her name, expecting to remember often her sweet disposition and the happy days spent near her." But by October, Audubon stridently maintains, "I believe I never laughed once with her the whole 4 months I was there." Two months after his firing, in a December 11, 1821, journal entry from New Orleans, Audubon mentions seeing Eliza on a city street and getting the brush-off: "My lovely Miss Pirrie of Oakley passed by me this morning, but did not remember how beautiful I had rendered her face once by painting it at her request with pastelles; she knew not the man who with the utmost patience and, in fact, attention, *waited* on her motions to please her—but thanks to my humble talents, I can run the gauntlet through this world without her help."

Interestingly, Eliza's presence on the street suggests that she had made a rebound from her convalescence, which her doctor had initially expected to take some months. The volatility of Audubon's attitude toward Eliza does very much resemble the roller coaster ride of a May-to-December romance. But Audubon could be quite moody, regardless of whether romance was in the equation. Drawn to the blithe moral certitudes of La Fontaine, Audubon seemed to view his personal and business relationships in stark black and white. He appeared to divide the world, somewhat peevishly, into those who were for him and those who were not.

Even Murphy, a great admirer of Audubon, is quick to point out his uneven disposition. "Do not infer that Audubon was without faults," Murphy cautions. "On the contrary, he was filled, in younger life at least, with a vanity little short of childish. He was tetchy, quick-tempered, inordinately moody, at times even vituperative." Said Dart, "He had an unfortunate inclination to bite the hand that fed him."

Professional pressures could have made Audubon more testy than usual at Oakley. Teaching was not his vocation, but a means to pay the bills while he pursued *The Birds of America.* His impatience with the demands of instruction is evident in his confession that he finished Eliza's work for her. His journals note various disagreements with other clients, such as the Heermans and the "Fair Incognito." Because we have only Audubon's side of the Oakley story, he's easily cast as a victim of the Pirries. While many or even all of the accusations he made against the Pirries may be true, it is also true that Audubon had a pattern of uneasy relationships with clients before and after the Pirries.

After his dismissal from Oakley, Audubon asked to stay as a guest at the plantation an additional eight to ten days to complete some of his bird studies. The Pirries agreed, and Audubon remained until October 20 under strained circumstances. This arrangement alone argues against any suggestion that Audubon was suspected of a scandalous relationship with Eliza. As Streshinsky has pointed out, if Audubon's dismissal had been prompted by such a concern, then surely the Pirries would not have hosted Audubon for more than a week after his dismissal.

Given the considerable evidence against any sexual connection between Audubon and Eliza, why does the legend persist? Audubon's vagueness about the circumstances of his departure from Oakley naturally invite speculation. "Fantasy floods in," playwright Peter Shaffer once observed, "where fact leaves a vacuum." Audubon's self-proclaimed motto, "Time will uncover the truth," has not, in this case, at least, seemed to apply. Nationally renowned naturalist Edward Hoagland has written that because naturalists tend to end up in lonely places in pursuit of their work, they're inevitably "pursued by rumors of romantic misconduct": "A special prurience attaches to inquiries as to whether Thoreau really fell in love with Emerson's wife, or why Audubon was abruptly exiled from Oakley Plantation in West Feliciana Parish, Louisiana, where he had been tutoring 'my lovely Miss Pirrie,' or whether poor Mrs. Hutchings, wife of [John] Muir's sawmill employer in Yosemite Valley, left her husband as a result of her winter's companionship with Muir."

Audubon and Eliza were probably not alone together long enough to

The fires of Oakley House's kitchen, located behind the main house, still burn today as a testament to the labors of the plantation's slaves.
Photo by Lori Waselchuk

The punkah fan overhead identifies this room as Oakley's dining room. The fan was typically operated by a slave child who moved the punkah by pulling a rope.
Photo by Lori Waselchuk

make a real dalliance possible. House has pointed out that it was custom-ary for young women such as Eliza to be followed by a "body servant," a slave who acted as a personal attendant. Such facts are easy to overlook, given the relative invisibility of slaves within Audubon's Oakley journal. Audubon's wages at Oakley came from a plantation economy that was, of course, built upon slave labor. In Oakley's dining room, an overhead punkah—a fan customarily pulled by a slave child—reminds visitors that Oakley's wealth and comfort came from an imprisoned work force. A slave exhibit behind the manor house stands as a reminder of the region's troubled racial history. Its presence invites questions about Audubon's attitudes toward slavery. Before coming to Oakley, Audubon had owned slaves in Kentucky, and his father had owned slaves in what is now Haiti. In an August 21, 1821, journal entry from Oakley, Audubon notes the tes-timony of local slaves that the flesh of the wood ibis is "excellent food."

In his *Ornithological Biography,* Audubon shares an anecdote about encountering a runaway slave and his family while birding in woods near St. Francisville. Audubon tells readers that he spent the night with the slave couple and their children, learning that they had fled various plan-tations after being separated for sale by their previous owner. Audubon recalls taking the frightened slaves back to their previous owner and ar-ranging for the family to remain intact. He ends on a note of self-congrat-ulation, assuring readers that the escapees "were rendered as happy as slaves generally are in that country, and continued to cherish that attach-ment to each other which had led to their adventures." Souder casts some doubts on this story, suggesting that it could be yet another of Audubon's tall tales. Souder wonders, for example, how a man of Audubon's low social standing during his Feliciana period could broker such generous conditions of amnesty with a local planter.

At the very least, the story suggests that Audubon wanted to be seen as tolerant of fellow human beings, even slaves. But it would be stretch-ing things to position Audubon as a liberal on matters of race. He seems to have accepted the notion of a hierarchy determined by skin color and expressed revulsion at New Orleans' racial intermingling. The "citron hue of almost all is very disgusting to one who likes the rosy Yankee or English cheeks," he writes from the Crescent City on January 14, 1821. John James Audubon, who delighted in the varied colors of birds, couldn't find beauty in a similar variety among people.

AUDUBON AFTER OAKLEY

When a disgruntled Audubon left Oakley House for New Orleans on October 20, 1821, he professed no regrets about leaving the Pirrie household. But Audubon did grieve about the woods he was leaving behind. Still smarting from his rift with the Pirries, he records leaving

> this abode of unfortunate opulence without a single sigh of regret . . . Not so with the sweet woods around us. To leave them was painful, for in them we always enjoyed peace and the sweetest pleasures of admiring the greatness of the Creator in all his unrivaled works. I often felt as if anxious to retain the fill of my lungs with the purer air that circulates through them, looked with pleasure and sorrow on the few virgin blooming magnolias—the three colored vines as we descended the hills of St. Francisville, and bid farewell to the country that, under different circumstances, we would have willingly divided with the ladies of Oakley.

Audubon's four months in the woods of Oakley had renewed his creative energies and given fresh momentum to *The Birds of America*. Audubon's interlude at Oakley "had been a period of marvelous productivity; he felt that he was progressing rapidly, and with steady money coming in, Lucy was no longer writing him contentious letters," Streshinsky observes.

In 2006 and early 2007, Dennis J. Dufrene, an interpretive ranger at the Audubon State Historic Site, undertook an extensive review of all 435 of the plates from *The Birds of America*. Determining the origins of Audubon's pictures can be tricky, since some of the artist's records are vague or nonexistent. Dufrene identified 23 pictures that Audubon either began or finished at Oakley, and another 16 pictures with possible links to Oakley. But Oakley's influence on Audubon was expressed not only in the quantity of his work, but in its quality.

During Audubon's Oakley stay, writes Carolyn DeLatte, his "journal entries seethed with excitement about the beautiful birds his sketches brought to life. The portfolio grew ever larger with the best drawings Audubon had yet created." For Audubon, Oakley also opened a door to birding wonders in other parts of Louisiana. Audubon began working on 167 (and possibly more) bird drawings while he was in Louisiana, according to the Louisiana State Museum in Baton Rouge. Audubon arrived in Louisiana in late 1820 and stayed in the state at various periods through 1837, Roulhac Toledano writes in *Audubon in Louisiana*. "However successful his various bird expeditions, he drew more birds for *The Birds of America* in Louisiana than in any other one place," Toledano adds.

"The State of Louisiana has always been my favorite portion of the Union, although Kentucky and some other States have divided my affections," Audubon wrote years later. Audubon's departure from Oakley didn't end his relationship with the Felicianas. By 1823, Lucy Audubon was working as a schoolmistress at West Feliciana's Beechwood Plantation, and John James and the Audubons' two sons were allowed to board there as well. But John James Audubon's relationship with Jane Percy, Beechwood's mistress, proved even more contentious than the one he had experienced with Lucretia Pirrie. Percy banished Audubon from the plantation at one point, though she allowed him to return and be nursed by Lucy after he and his son Victor were stricken with yellow fever. In the twenty-three months that he spent in the Felicianas during periodic visits, Audubon worked on at least eighty of the birds in the elephant edition of *The Birds of America*, according to Dart.

Lucy Audubon's teaching positions at Beechwood and, later, nearby Beech Grove Plantation provided a crucial source of family income as John James Audubon set sail for England in 1826 to advance *The Birds of America*. England, still the world's dominant political, economic, and technological center in the 1820s, was the logical place for Audubon to seek the financial and technical support necessary for his ambitious project. In 1829, after the first forty-nine plates of *The Birds of America* had appeared, the *American Journal of Science and Arts* hailed it as "the most magnificent work of its kind ever executed in any country." Many others agreed, and Audubon was well on his way to becoming an international sensation.

In 1838, with Oakley House now in the hands of his former student, Eliza, Audubon looked toward his own matters of succession. His principal legacy, *The Birds of America,* was complete, and as he entered advanced age, Audubon was more deeply involving his sons, Victor and John Woodhouse Audubon, in the family business.

In 1840, with help from John Woodhouse, Audubon embarked upon an octavo version of *The Birds of America*—a smaller format that would extend his popular bird studies to a broader audience and include text similar to that of his *Ornithological Biography.* The venture made a sizable profit and enabled Audubon to pay for Minniesland, a handsome New York estate. It was there, on January 27, 1851, that Audubon died after declining into dementia.

Pioneering a business strategy that would anticipate the modern-day franchising of creative properties, Audubon was becoming not just a man, but a brand. Although the phenomenon would not reach its real potential until Audubon's sons had also passed from the scene, Audubon's legacy would, over time, emerge as a major industry of Audubon books, prints, calendars, and stationery. In 1905, the National Association of Audubon Societies was incorporated in New York. George Grinnell, who had pioneered the building of the Audubon Society in the late 1800s, had been a student of Lucy Audubon.

Could Audubon have succeeded without his Oakley period? As Murphy has observed, once Audubon embraced the concept of *The Birds of America*, "no trial was sufficient to make him swerve a half-point from his course. For that cause, he not only suffered cold, homelessness, raggedness, hunger, and their attendant despondency, but even far sharper punishment of the contempt of men for his condition." Even so, Oakley provided financial support and a wealth of subjects at a pivotal time in Audubon's artistic development. "I think it rescued him as a man in his intent to paint *The Birds of America*," said Dart. "Oakley provided him not only with a place to paint birds, and the wherewithal, but a certain amount of freedom."

Audubon found inspiration in many places. No single locale can contain the sum of who he was. But Audubon's bird pictures freeze the flux of life in an instant of time and space, carefully recreating not only how a creature lives but, through verdant backgrounds, where it lives. The message here, quite clearly, is that place defines us. The same is true of people, too. We can look at Audubon's Oakley period the way an archaeologist might mull over an old shard of pottery, using a bright fragment of the past to reveal a larger whole. After all, Audubon's stay at Oakley can seem a sort of distillation of the themes that followed him throughout his life—the anxious angling for money, the ecstasy of art, the entanglement of scandal, and the quest for fame.

OAKLEY AFTER AUDUBON

Only a few years after he left Oakley, Audubon's fame flourished. Meanwhile, back at Oakley House, change came more slowly. To the casual observer, Oakley after Audubon might seem like one of those enchanted kingdoms that fall into a deep sleep after the favored prince suffers exile. But even at Oakley, time marched on, however imperceptibly. Eliza Pirrie married for the first time in 1823. As with her earlier connection with Audubon, the experience created a legend of romantic scandal touched by the tragic. According to Oakley's official history, Eliza eloped with Robert Hilliard Barrow, a local planter's son, after Eliza's parents refused to give them permission to marry. Robert Barrow died six weeks later. According to the local lore, he had fallen ill after carrying Eliza across a nearby stream on the night of their elopement. Their short union produced a son, Robert Hilliard Barrow, Jr.

James Pirrie died a year later, in 1824, and Lucretia Pirrie, who had earned distinction before their marriage for running Oakley as a widow, was once again in charge of the plantation. Lucretia survived James by nearly a decade, passing away in 1833. Like many plantation homes near

St. Francisville, Oakley's manor house remained intact through the Civil War, though the conclusion of the war and the end of slavery brought big changes to the cotton economy that had created the Pirries' wealth.

Even so, when Stanley Clisby Arthur commemorated the centennial of Audubon's arrival at Oakley by retracing Audubon's path on June 18, 1921, he was struck by how little had changed:

> Making the identical pilgrimage, I could picture the artist's delight in the woodland scenes that lay on every side of the long twisting road that led to *Oakley*. The magnolia trees were in bloom, the holly and the beech trees were covered with verdant leaves, the slim yellow poplars reached high into the blue and cloud-flecked sky above the hilly ground and red clay. I, too, like Audubon, was surrounded on every side by warblers and thrushes making the soft summer air glad with their chorus. Treading the same route, at the same time of the year, I could easily comprehend Audubon's instant infatuation with this truly beautiful region. From every shrub and every bush and every tree the birds sang their nuptial lays, as their gaudily colored forms flitted from branch to branch and tree to tree. A bird paradise, one indeed beyond compare.

Ironically, Louisiana's lag behind much of the country in economic progress had helped to insulate the Felicianas from at least some development pressures as Arthur made his centennial walk. But elsewhere, in many other parts of the nation, America was coming into its own as an industrial superpower. With that transition had come increasing concern about the effects of growth on the environment.

Audubon's stature—and his important connection with Oakley—wasn't lost on the Pirrie descendants as the plantation passed from generation to generation. After Lucretia's death in 1833, Eliza inherited Oakley. Eliza's second husband, the Rev. William Robert Bowman, whom she had married in 1828, died in 1835. Eliza died in 1851—ironically, the same year as Audubon—passing ownership of Oakley to her third husband, Henry Lyons. Lyons sold Oakley to his son-in-law, William Matthews,

Lucy Matthews, the last of the
Pirrie descendants to live at
Oakley House
*Photo provided by Audubon
State Historic Site*

A picture believed to be of
Ida Matthews
*Photo provided by Audubon
State Historic Site*

who was married to Isabelle, a daughter from Eliza's second marriage. After William and Isabelle Matthews died near the dawn of the twentieth century, Oakley was owned by their daughters, Lucy and Ida Matthews, who didn't marry.

Though Audubon's visit to Oakley was a distant memory by the time Ida was born, she shared many of the artistic interests of Oakley's most famous resident, dabbling in painting and writing, and trying unsuccessfully to get published, despite some modest encouragement from Ambrose Bierce. Renowned for his sharp literary tongue, Bierce nevertheless wrote a thoughtful and diplomatic response to Ida's apparent request for assistance in becoming a writer. "There can be no question of your literary gifts," Bierce writes in a March 5, 1906, letter. "It is manifest, even through the signs (abundant enough) of your lack of knowledge of the arts. But you must understand that literature is an art—a most difficult one, not to be acquired without long and hard technical study, as well as by close reading of the masters . . . The poet's vocation is no couch of roses, but I hope you may not find it a bed of coals."

Like Audubon, Ida had a flair for the unconventional, undertaking an earnest study of African American spiritual music in a time and place where black culture was routinely dismissed as inferior. Her final flouting of convention came in 1930, when, honoring a request she had made before her death, a number of Oakley's black tenants acted as pallbearers at her funeral.

Lucy Matthews, the last of the Pirrie line to occupy Oakley, entered a nursing home in 1942. Audubon's fame had been established for more than a century, so it seemed natural that the state of Louisiana would be interested in acquiring Oakley as a public historic site. The state bought Oakley House and the surrounding one hundred acres from the original plantation operation for $10,000 in 1947. It took state officials seven years to inventory and prepare the house, which had remained substantially unchanged since Audubon's day, still without electricity and running water, and which included a wealth of family pictures and documents. Lucy Matthews died in 1952.

Even before Oakley opened to the public in 1954, Audubon was

A hostess sweeps the porch of Oakley House shortly before the start of a tour.
Photo by Lori Waselchuk

known, as the writer Katherine Anne Porter said, as the area's "most treasured inhabitant" and "its happiest memory." In her 1939 travelogue of
the Felicianas, Porter celebrated the region as largely removed from the
vulgarities of modern commerce. Except for "the fruits of the earth" and
a few postcards for sale at nearby Rosedown Plantation, Porter lauded
Audubon country as a place where "there was nothing, really nothing,
for sale." But the commercial possibilities of the Audubon legend would
not be lost on the locals indefinitely, as evidenced by the emergence of
Feliciana convenience stores, real estate companies, and other establish-
ments bearing Audubon's name. Because of Audubon's legacy, Oakley
and its environs have beckoned as not only a tourist attraction, but a
literary touchstone.

Nearly two decades after Porter's visit, Robert Penn Warren tapped
Oakley as a source for his 1957 poem cycle, "Audubon: A Vision." In 1976,
as America was looking with renewed scrutiny upon its racial past, Edward Hoagland published "Virginie and the Slaves," a probing travelogue
in which he comments on Oakley's dual position as an Audubon site and

former place of bondage: "On the walls are Audubon's chipping spar-row, tufted duck, red-cockaded woodpecker, and cerulean warbler, and there are leather fire buckets, pewter plates (called 'poor man's silver'), a spinning-and-weaving room, and an inventory of slaves, in which I no-ticed that a man in his forties like me was still considered to be worth the top price of seven hundred dollars, as were others ten years younger or even just nineteen." In 2000, lending an eloquent voice to the themes only suggested in Hoagland's essay, anthropologist Laurie A. Wilkie pub-lished *Creating Freedom,* a provocative look at African American life at Oakley.

A generation earlier, in 1980, Mary Durant and Michael Harwood had published *On the Road with John James Audubon,* a retracing of the des-tinations in Audubon's journal. Harwood, whose commentary alternates with Durant's throughout the book, visited Oakley and wondered how the changing times would influence Audubon's old stomping grounds:

> Time marches on, all right. Just downstream from Bayou Sara and St. Francisville, Gulf States Utilities is building a nuclear power plant—with fearful urgency. There has been some opposition to the project in the parish, we understand, but it's not enough so far to bring things to a halt. Tonight, having seen bright lights in that neighborhood from the ferry landing, and later hearing the roar of distant engines as we finished supper, we put two and two to-gether and went to investigate. It turns out the contractor is work-ing nights to get the nuke built. From a bridge at what must be the fringe of the site, we watched monstrous earthmoving equipment grinding across freshly flattened and graded earth, in the glare of floodlights.

St. Francisville's nuclear power plant has operated without incident since Harwood's speculation about its effect on Oakley's home parish, but subsequent development has made Oakley increasingly less isolated than the refuge Audubon found in 1821. Not surprisingly, many of the same things that drew Audubon to West Feliciana, such as its clear air and nat-

ural beauty, have made it attractive for residential growth. In 2006, builders broke ground for a new bridge spanning the Mississippi and connect-
ing St. Francisville with the nearby community of New Roads. Business
leaders and others predicted that the bridge would create an economic
boom for both sides of the river, including Audubon's old haunts. Ironically enough, the project was named the John James Audubon Bridge.

In spite of the changes, Audubon would still find many birds to draw
if he returned to the Felicianas today. The grounds around Oakley are
thick with loblolly pine, red oak, water oak, live oak, and sweet gum,
among other species. Understory vegetation, such as cherry laurel, dog-
wood, yaupon, wild hydrangea, and French mulberry, is also a big draw
for birds. The nearby Port Hudson State Commemorative Area, located
on the site of a Civil War battle, offers about seven miles of trails that
feature an abundance of birds. Hikes through nearby Tunica Hills create
other opportunities for birders.

"Birds of the Felicianas," a birding checklist issued by the Department
of Culture, Recreation, and Tourism's Office of State Parks, features more
than 150 species that bird-watchers can expect to find in the area at various times of the year. While not meant to be all-inclusive, the list hints
at the region's continuing ecological bounty. It includes everything from
the downy woodpecker, which Audubon praised as "not surpassed by
any of its tribe in hardiness, industry, or vivacity," to the great blue heron,
which Audubon found "extremely suspicious and shy," to the pine warbler,
whose flight impressed Audubon with its "undulating curves of considerable elegance."

But Audubon would also find marked absences in the natural landscape of the Felicianas if he returned. The most obvious change, of course,
would be the vast reduction in natural habitat. "The forest that he would
see would be a different one than the one he knew," said Keith Ouchley,
Louisiana director of The Nature Conservancy. At the time of European
settlement, the bottomland hardwood forests of the Mississippi River
delta spanned some 24 million acres. During Audubon's Oakley visit, the
forest system would have remained vast. Today, according to the Conser-

vancy, the delta's 24-million-acre expanse of bottomland hardwood forests stands at just 4.4 million acres. "He would be greatly disappointed," Ouchley said of Audubon.

The red-cockaded woodpecker that created so much excitement in Audubon's bedroom at Oakley would find few descendants in the area today, remarked Ouchley. "To my knowledge, it may never again have been recorded in this area," added Ouchley, noting that the bird tends to prefer open, parklike pinelands rather than hardwoods. The birds like to nest in older pines, and with the modern efficiencies of foresting, "we just don't let [the trees] get that old before harvesting." Because of such challenges, the red-cockaded woodpecker has now been placed on the federal list of endangered species. "If Audubon shot one today, he could get arrested," Ouchley said.

On a more hopeful note, Ouchley said that the American redstart and the Louisiana waterthrush, two birds that Audubon drew at Oakley, can still be heard "throughout the spring and summer calling out from the cool, shaded ravines" near Oakley. "The waterthrush in particular is very closely tied to the clear sandy streams, where it walks along the creek bed, bobbing its tail as it forages," he noted. "No doubt this habitat was more prevalent in Audubon's day, and land clearing and forest fragmentation have decreased the availability of the forests for this species."

The 2005 arrival of Hurricane Katrina portended greater development pressures on Oakley's home parish of West Feliciana as a scrambled housing market made the Felicianas even more attractive to prospective new residents. Significantly, the storm left Oakley intact, though international publicity about Louisiana's hurricane damage brought a drop in visitors to the Audubon State Historic Site. Even so, a little more than a year after Katrina's landfall, Oakley's supporters honored its past—and looked toward the future—with a September 23, 2006, celebration of Oakley House's two-hundredth birthday.

Rain threatened on the horizon as members of the Daughters of the American Revolution, adorned with festive hats, gathered under Oakley's oaks to sing "Happy Birthday," share birthday cake, and recall the DAR's

Members of the Daughters of the American Revolution gathered on September 23, 2006, to mark the two-hundredth birthday of Oakley House.
Photo by Lori Waselchuk

role in lobbying for the state's 1947 purchase of Oakley, a move that preserved it for future generations. The rain held off for the morning, leaving the red, white, and blue bunting across Oakley's top story high and dry. It was the kind of day that Audubon, a fan of great parties, might have enjoyed. Audubon's old rift with the Pirries seemed forgiven as Pirrie relatives Anne B. Klein and Ann Stirling Weller came to the outdoor podium to share in the birthday celebration.

Klein, in an interview after the ceremony, recalled living for a time in Evansville, Indiana, not far from Audubon's former home in Henderson, Kentucky. While Audubon's connection to Henderson was well known among the locals, "none of them had ever heard of St. Francisville," she said with amusement. Klein is proud of her family and her community's link with Audubon. As Oakley entered a new century, renewed national interest in Audubon's life, as evidenced by a surge of new Audubon books, promised to bring more attention to Oakley and its unique connection with the artist.

Weller recalled the work of her mother, Josie Landry Stirling, in helping to lobby state officials to buy the old house as a historic property, and
later serving as Oakley's first curator. Weller credited two local sisters,
Farah and Mamie Butler, for conceiving the idea of preserving Oakley as
a historic site. "It was deteriorating, and it had been for years," Weller said
of Oakley's condition shortly before the sale. But with state acquisition
came the resources to save Oakley for future generations.

There seemed little question, of course, that the state would designate
Oakley as the Audubon State Historic Site. Audubon stayed at Oakley
only four months, a tiny fraction of its two-hundred-year history. But
as Oakley marked its first two centuries, he remained its principal star.
Audubon's story of Oakley, the one recorded in his journal, was the one
the world would remember.

AUDUBON'S OAKLEY LEGACY

Writers stamp themselves on houses, "making the table, the chair, the
carpet into their own image," Virginia Woolf once observed. In just such
a way, John James Audubon had used the English language to write a star-
ring role for himself in Oakley's history. But it was Audubon's pictures,
more than his journal, that guaranteed a place for himself and Oakley for
the ages.

A short drive from Oakley, at LSU's Hill Memorial Library, a great
double elephant folio of Audubon's *Birds of America* commands special
stature as one of the library's most valuable treasures. Once a year, the
four-volume set, once owned by the Duke of Northumberland, makes
a public appearance during Hill's Audubon Day. Wearing gloves, staff
members slowly turn all of the pages, from start to finish, then start over
again. As many as 120 people register in advance for the three-hour viewing. "Some people stay for 30 minutes, some stay for two hours," said
Elaine B. Smyth, Hill's head of special collections.

Audubon's bird pictures are among the most reproduced art images in
the world—staples of Web sites, calendars, posters, and prints for mass

consumption. In spite of their mass-market ubiquity—or perhaps because of it—the images beg to be seen as they were when they first came off the press. "Reproductions often look very 'flat' both in texture and in color, compared to the originals," said Smyth. "Visual quality aside, there is also the historical aspect—the difference between a print that was created approximately 170 years ago and one that was created more recently."

Given Audubon's unique standing as the patron saint of American ornithology, Hill's Audubon Day can seem like a religious ceremony. More than a century and a half after his death, Audubon's work continues to inspire the admiration of modern-day bird artists. "He is a true master at creating texture, and his works are incredible," said internationally known bird artist John O'Neill. "To see an original Audubon painting is an amazing experience."

Such praise can convey a sense of supreme summation, as if Audubon finished the story of American bird life. Visitors can get a similar feeling as they close their tour of Oakley House, which concludes on the manor's gallery. From the upper floor of Oakley, this world once walked by Audubon can seem as comfortably self-contained as a snow globe. But the Audubon legacy memorialized at Oakley isn't the snapped ribbon of a finish line, but a baton in an ongoing race. Audubon dramatically advanced bird art, but he didn't perfect it, and no artist ever does. Even O'Neill, an avowed Audubon fan, acknowledges the master's limitations. "Since he painted birds life-sized, he sometimes put large birds into somewhat unconventional poses, but even these are exceedingly well-done," said O'Neill.

The late Roger Tory Peterson, whose line of field guides brought birdwatching to the masses after World War II, knew that to really appreciate Audubon, a man who stood as a hero for Peterson, it was necessary to understand Audubon's shortfalls. "Audubon wired up his specimens, and they sometimes looked it," Peterson writes in a 1981 edition of *The Birds of America*. "His two blue-winged teal look as though they were thrown through the air like footballs." But Audubon's work lacks perfection not only because of his personal limitations, but because ornithology, like all sciences, still contains frontiers.

O'Neill, who has earned distinction for his groundbreaking orni-thological studies in Peru, once said: "Peru has been my Louisiana, my Oakley Plantation." O'Neill's comment reminds us that Oakley is less a piece of geography than a state of mind, the promise of new terrains to dazzle the eye and stretch the mind. With that comes the hope that there will always be an Oakley, even after the last bricks of this old plantation have crumbled back into the land where John James Audubon found "the sweetest pleasures of admiring the greatness of the Creator in all his un-rivaled works."

Bonaparte Flycatcher (Modern name: Canada Warbler). As noted by Roger Tory Peterson, Audubon named this bird after Prince Charles-Lucien Bonaparte. Ornithologists have determined that it is not a flycatcher, but a young female Canada warbler.

Selby's Flycatcher (Modern name: Hooded Warbler). Audubon thought this was a new species when he encountered it at Oakley, so he named it after a British ornithologist, Prideaux John Selby. Actually, it was an immature hooded warbler, states Peterson.

The hooded warbler, which gets its name from its distinctive cowl, remains a spring and summer visitor to Louisiana. *Photo courtesy of Louisiana Department of Wildlife and Fisheries*

Prairie Warbler. Peterson noted that Audubon erred in depicting this bird on a sedge drawn by Joseph Mason. It typically likes other kinds of vegetation.

Bewick's Long-tailed Wren (Modern name: Bewick's Wren). In the octavo edition of his *Birds of America,* Audubon says he killed this specimen near St. Francisville on October 19, 1821. According to his journal, he left Oakley the following day.

Louisiana Waterthrush. "Much and justly as the song of the nightingale is admired, I am inclined, after having listened to it, to pronounce it in no degree superior to that of the Louisiana water thrush," Audubon wrote in *Birds of America,* octavo edition.

Mockingbird (Modern name: Northern Mockingbird). Audubon's dramatic depiction of mockingbirds being attacked by a rattlesnake provoked a controversy that dogged him for years. Many doubted the scenario pictured in the painting, as well as Audubon's other claims about rattlesnakes.

Alexander Wilson's depiction of a mockingbird (top) is much more sedate than Audubon's, evidence of the bird artists' markedly different styles. Audubon's spectacular bird pictures would eventually overshadow those of Wilson among the viewing public.

In Audubon's time as today, the mockingbird was a fixture of Louisiana's landscape. *Photo courtesy of Louisiana Department of Wildlife and Fisheries*

Roscoe's Yellow-throat (Modern name: Common Yellowthroat). Believing it was a new species, Audubon named this bird after English historian William Roscoe, Peterson notes. It appears to be a common yellowthroat.

Children's Warbler (Modern name: Yellow Warbler). This is actually a female and immature yellow warbler. Peterson states that Audubon initially thought he had found a new species, naming it after John George Children, a secretary of the Royal Society of London.

American Redstart. The redstart is a spring and summer visitor to the Felicianas and can still be found in the area, according to Keith Ouchley, state director of The Nature Conservancy.

Here, a Louisiana Department of Wildlife and Fisheries staffer holds a redstart as part of a conservation program. *Photo courtesy of Louisiana Department of Wildlife and Fisheries*

Summer Red Bird (Modern name: Summer Tanager). The bird's brilliant color seems tailor-made for an Audubon print. It can still be found in the Felicianas.

Blue-green Warbler (Modern name: Cerulean Warbler). In the octavo edition of his *Birds of America,* Audubon corrected his assertion that the blue-green warbler was a separate species. What he saw was probably a female or a young male cerulean warbler.

Black and Yellow Warbler (Modern name: Magnolia Warbler), erroneously labeled "Swainson's Warbler" by the engraver. "Few of our warblers have a more varied plumage, or are more animated, than this beautiful little bird," Audubon observed in *Birds of America,* octavo edition. He drew the bird on October 20, 1821—the day he left Oakley.

Swallow-tailed Hawk (Modern name: Swallow-tailed Kite). Audubon's powerful depiction of this swallow-tailed kite is considered among his finest works. The bird's numbers likely declined around Oakley as local swamps were drained for agriculture, according to Keith Ouchley.

Indigo Bird (Modern name: Indigo Bunting). Its brilliant blue plumage made a stunning picture when Audubon captured the indigo bunting during his stay at Oakley. Audubon noted in his journal that it was "tolerably plenty."

The indigo bunting remains in the area and is a favorite among modern-day Louisiana birders. *Photo courtesy of Louisiana Department of Wildlife and Fisheries*

Yellow-throat Warbler (Modern name: Yellow-throated Warbler). "As it is heard in all parts of our most dismal cypress swamps, it contributes to soothe the mind of a person whose occupation may lead him to such places," Audubon wrote of this bird in *Birds of America,* octavo edition.

Mississippi Kite. Many of those who follow Audubon's work believe that Audubon's engraver, Robert Havell, copied the kite depicted on the lower branch *(left)* from an illustration made by Audubon's rival, Alexander Wilson *(right, center)*, in order to fill out Audubon's bird plate. Notice the stiffness of the bird on the lower branch, which is strikingly similar to Wilson's. The dynamism of the bird on the upper branch is much more typical of Audubon's style.

The spectral image of the Mississippi kite commands attention even today in Audubon's old stomping grounds around Oakley Plantation. It's a summer visitor to the region. *Photo courtesy of Louisiana Department of Wildlife and Fisheries*

Yellow-throated Vireo. Audubon was fond of assigning moral qualities to birds, as with his thoughts on the yellow-throated vireo. In *Birds of America,* octavo edition, he praises this vireo as a "slow, careful and industrious bird," much unlike the "petulant" and "infantile" white-eyed vireo.

Pine Creeping Warbler (Modern name: Pine Warbler). In *Birds of America,* octavo edition, Audubon admires the flight of the pine warbler for its "undulating curves of considerable elegance."

Tennessee Warbler. The Tennessee warbler can still be heard singing from treetops in West Feliciana Parish during its spring migration, according to Keith Ouchley. "It prefers forests over fields, and land clearing would not be beneficial to this species," says Ouchley.

White Ibis. Audubon spotted a white ibis grooming itself at Oakley and, as he noted in his journal, watched as "it sat a long time arranging its feathers using its scythe-shaped bill very dexterously."

Pied Oyster-catcher (Modern name: American Oystercatcher). Research conducted by the Audubon State Historic Site concluded that Audubon worked on a picture of the oystercatcher while at Oakley. Although the oystercatcher is a coastal bird, it is possible that Audubon used a bird skin he had brought to Oakley for his subject.

Spotted Sandpiper. Bayou Sara near Oakley Plantation figures into the background of this nature scene. The evidence suggests that Audubon worked on the picture in August 1821, according to Dennis J. Dufrene.

Red-cockaded Woodpecker. Audubon captured two red-cockaded woodpeckers during his Oakley period and brought them back to Oakley House for observation. One died in transit, and the other one held court in his bedroom. The red-cockaded woodpecker is now an endangered species.

In addition to the 23 plates from *Birds of America* that Dennis J. Dufrene has linked to Audubon's time at Oakley, there are 16 other plates that Dufrene thinks may have a connection, though he deemed the evidence inconclusive. Those pictures follow. They appear to have originated in or around 1821, and might have been conceived elsewhere in Louisiana.

Yellow-billed Cuckoo

Prothonotary Warbler

Carolina Parrot (Modern name: Carolina Parakeet)

Golden-winged Woodpecker (Modern name: Northern Flicker)

Barred Owl

Red-tailed Hawk

Chipping Sparrow

Summer or Wood Duck (Modern name: Wood Duck)

Great Blue Heron

Mallard

Great Esquimaux Curlew (Modern name: Whimbrel)

Pied-billed Dobchick (Modern name: Pied-billed Grebe)

Red-breasted Sandpiper (Modern name: Red Knot)

Lesser Tern (Modern Name: Least Tern)

Yellow-breasted Rail (Modern name: Yellow Rail)

Green Heron

Notes

Oakley Overture

1 History is interesting: David McCullough, interview with author, March 1995.

2 "In 1821, the annual per capita Gross Domestic Product": Samuel H. Williamson, e-mail message to author, June 21, 2007. More information about understanding historical financial data in contemporary terms is available at a Web site created by Williamson and fellow scholar Lawrence H. Officer: www.measuringworth.com.

2 "drawing, music, dancing": Irmscher, ed., *John James Audubon: Writings and Drawings*, 124.

2 "a revelation": Souder, *Under a Wild Sky*, 185.

2 "a paradise of birds": Rhodes, *John James Audubon: The Making of an American*, 199.

2 "His time at Oakley": O'Neill, "Studying and Painting Birds: Audubon's Time Vs. Today," in Dormon, ed., *Audubon: A Retrospective*, 94.

4 "bird heaven": Arthur, *Audubon: An Intimate Life of the American Woodsman*, 197.

4 "was as luxuriant in bird life": Streshinsky, *Audubon: Life and Art in the American Wilderness*, 129.

4 "an abode of unfortunate opulence": *Writings and Drawings*, 128.

6 At one point he claimed: Maria R. Audubon, ed., *Audubon and His Journals*, Vol. 1, p. 5.

7 The U.S. economic reverse: *The Making of an American*, 132.

9 As Audubon related the development: Ibid., 193.

9 "As he had done his whole adult life": *Under a Wild Sky*, 259.

10 St. Francisville resident: Al Troy, conversation with author, April 29, 2006.

11 "in rich houses": Warren, *The Collected Poems of Robert Penn Warren*, 264.

"The Hawk That Poises in the Air"

11 "We were awakened last night": *Writings and Drawings*, 115.

12 "that a clergyman": Ibid., 864.

12 "Audubon was the greatest slayer of birds that ever lived": Blotner, *Robert Penn Warren*, 382.

13 Less than an hour's drive: Van Remsen, e-mail message to author, October 30, 2006.

13 "Granted, a scientist needs specimens": Irmscher, *The Poetics of Natural History*, 207.

14 "the protector and slayer of birds": Ibid., 217.

14 Rhodes suggests: *Making of an American*, 22.

14 "many of Audubon's compositions": *Poetics of Natural History*, 221.

14 "Absent for a long period": Keith Ouchley, e-mail message to author, January 22, 2007.

15 "time flies, nature loses": Murphy, *John James Audubon (1785–1851): An Evaluation*, 348.

15 "It has been suggested": *Robert Penn Warren*, 385.

15 Eudora Welty, who had inspired: Marrs, *Eudora Welty*, 345.

15 "the transitory": Welty, *A Writer's Eye*, 223.

15 Just a month before arriving: *Life and Art in the American Wilderness*, 127.

The Pirries of Oakley

16 In 1781, when Lucretia: *Oakley House Tour Manual*.

17 Three years earlier: Ibid.

18 Five of the six children: *Writings and Drawings*, 126.

18 "generous . . . but giving way for want": Ibid., 125.

18 "an extraordinary woman": Ibid.

18 "We were called *good* men": *Writings and Drawings*, 124.

19 "a man of strong mind": Ibid., 125.

20 Souder writes that: *Under a Wild Sky*, 187.

John James Audubon Slept Here

23 "He immediately reviewed": *Writings and Drawings*, 113–14.

23 "about 18 years of age": Ibid., 3.

24 an omission that offended Mason: *Life and Art in the American Wilderness*, 151.

24 "Audubon biographers who are": Bannon, "The Audubon Prints," in Dormon, ed., *Audubon: A Retrospective*, 62.

24 taller than the period average: *Making of an American*, 5.

"The Country Entirely New to Us"

25 joked in his journal: *Writings and Drawings*, 103.

25 "The aspect of the country": Ibid., 104.

26 "New Orleans to a man": *Audubon and His Journals*, Vol. 1, p. 81.

26 Audubon related the story: Irmscher, "Audubon and the Veiled Lady," 68–72.

26 It was here that: *Writings and Drawings*, 865.

27 The geography of the Felicianas: Ouchley, interview with author, October 25, 2006.

27 "very abundant": *Writings and Drawings*, 104–11.

27 "Was deceived one day": Ibid., 105.

28 "Judging by his description": Peterson and Peterson, eds., *Audubon's Birds of America*, introduction.

Audubon's Rival

28 As Souder points out: *Under a Wild Sky*, 11–12.

29 "Whatever Audubon thought or said": Ibid., 271.

29 "the egg represented by Wilson": *Writings and Drawings*, 107.

29 "I have many times": Ibid.

29 "the figure of Wilson": Ibid., 105.

29 "the great many errors": Ibid., 126.

An Audubon Fourth

30 During the region's period of Spanish rule: John R. House III, interview with author, September 30, 2006.

30 One of his most memorable stretches: Rhodes, *The Audubon Reader*, 17–20.

31 It seems nothing more than an accident: Thoreau, *Walden*, 358.

32 "the weather sultry": *Writings and Drawings*, 115.

32 "Weather since Monday": Ibid., 99–100.

32 "a hot, sultry day": Ibid., 104.

32 an often fatal illness: "Yellow Fever Deaths in New Orleans."

32 "cases of yellow fever": *Writings and Drawings*, 100.

33 "During untold hours": *Audubon in Louisiana*, introduction.

33 Site manager House notes that: House, interview with author, September 30, 2006.

Bird-Watching in Audubon's Footsteps

35 "Do you hear that weeping?": Cathy Troy, conversation with author, April 29, 2006.

35 "The squeak": Audubon, *Birds of America* (online), http://www.audubon.org/bird/BoA/F7_G2d.html.

36 "mournful whinny": Peterson, *Birds of Eastern and Central North America*, 202.

36 "Who could imagine": *Writings and Drawings*, 288.

36 "He is more tyrannical": Ibid., 291.

37 "Last April": Ibid., 104.

37 "I had the pleasure of meeting": Ibid., 113.

40 "You could not ask for": Troy, conversation with author, April 29, 2006.

An Audubon Repast

41 "As someone in St. Francisville": Durant and Harwood, *On the Road with John James Audubon*, 229.

41 "the nineteenth-century version": House, interview with author, September 30, 2006.

41 "a really true philosopher": *Writings and Drawings*, 125.

41 House likes to remind visitors: House, interview with author, September 30, 2006.

42 Audubon passed a rainy morning: *Writings and Drawings*, 28–33.

43 Audubon's editor: *Audubon's Birds of America*, introduction.

John James Audubon, Oakley Scribe

43 "We are all familiar with": Sanders, *Audubon Reader*, 1.

44 As Sanders reminds readers: Ibid., 1–2.

44 So the reader is not surprised: *Writings and Drawings*, 63.

44 Jean de La Fontaine: La Fontaine, *Selected Fables*, title page synopsis.

45 "the very dawn of": McClatchy, ed., *On Wings of Song*, 13.

46 "Anxious to give it": *Writings and Drawings*, 123.

46 "species of snakes ascend": Ibid., 230.

46 "rattlesnakes can climb": American International Rattlesnake Museum Web site, http://www.rattlesnakes.com/items/item09.html.

47 He tells of a snake: *Under a Wild Sky*, 223–24.

47 Audubon's scientific paper: Chalmers, *Audubon in Edinburgh*, 142.

47 "Audubon was not one to allow": Ibid., 136.

Audubon's Oakley Hunting Ground

47 "Audubon was presumably": *Audubon: An Evaluation*, 335.

47 lavish shipments of salmon: Rachel Scharff, facsimile transmission to author, January 25, 2007.

48 "They ate game": House, interview with author, September 30, 2006.

48 "the chuck will's widow": *Writings and Drawings*, 111.

48 "Dead-Eye Dick": *Audubon: An Evaluation*, 319.

48 "He was a man's man": Elisabeth Dart, interview with author, January 13, 2007.

49 "Henry David Thoreau": Abbey, *One Life at a Time, Please*, 38.

49 "John James Audubon, who can stir": *Audubon: An Evaluation*, 346.

49 "In Audubon's own day," *Audubon Reader*, 7.

49 "millions of golden plovers": *Writings and Drawings*, 87.

50 "Apologists for Audubon's industrial-style killings": *Poetics of Natural History*, 214.

50 "Audubon, too, recognized": *Audubon in Edinburgh*, 134.

50 "Audubon's real contribution": Peterson and Peterson, eds., *Audubon's Birds of America*, introduction.

A Pained Farewell

51 "were spent in peaceable": *Writings and Drawings*, 124.

51 "No doubt much too much": Ibid., 126.

51 "the *man she loved*": Ibid.

52 "I saw her": Ibid.

52 "was then laboring": *Writings and Drawings*, 127.

52 "the grossest words of insult": Ibid.

53 "Toward summer's end": Ford, *John James Audubon*, 130.

53 "took note—perhaps not appropriately": *Under a Wild Sky*, 187.

53 "Miss P. had no": *Writings and Drawings*, 125.

54 "anxious to know him": Ibid., 104.

54 "He *was* a flirt": *Life and Art in the American Wilderness*, 134.

54 Just before his arrival at Oakley: *Making of an American*, 195.

54 "deftly doctored to stir up": "Audubon and the Veiled Lady," 68.

55 "To judge from the abundant": *Audubon: An Evaluation*, 323.

55 "my amiable pupil": *Writings and Drawings*, 124.

55 "I believe I never": Ibid., 126.

55 "My lovely Miss Pirrie": Ibid., 145.

55 "some months" : Ibid., 126.

55 "Do not infer": *Audubon: An Evaluation*, 319.

55 "He had an unfortunate": Dart, interview with author, January 13, 2007.

56 he finished Eliza's work: *Writings and Drawings*, 125.

56 as a guest at the plantation: Ibid., 126.

56 As Streshinsky has pointed out: *Life and Art in the American Wilderness*, 135.

56 "Fantasy floods in": Shaffer, *Lettice and Lovage*, 25.

56 "Time will uncover": *An Intimate Life of the American Woodsman*, title page.

56 "pursued by rumors": Hoagland, *Hoagland on Nature*, 452.

58 it was customary: House, interview with author, September 30, 2006.

58 "excellent food": *Writings and Drawings*, 123.

58 "were rendered as happy": De Caro and Jordan, eds., *Louisiana Sojourns*, 194.

58 Souder wonders: *Under a Wild Sky*, 262.

58 "citron hue of almost all": *Writings and Drawings*, 77.

Audubon after Oakley

59 "this abode of unfortunate": *Writings and Drawings*, 128.

59 "had been a period of marvelous": *Life and Art in the American Wilderness*, 135.

59 In 2006 and early 2007: Dennis J. Dufrene, e-mail message to author, December 19, 2006.

60 "journal entries seethed": DeLatte, *Lucy Audubon: A Biography*, 117.

60 "However successful": Toledano, in *Audubon in Louisiana*.

60 "The State of Louisiana": *Birds of America* (online), http://www.audubon.org/bird/BoA/F38_G1g.html.

60 In the twenty-three months: Dart, interview with author, January 13, 2007.

61 "the most magnificent": *Writings and Drawings*, 866.

61 "no trial was sufficient": *Audubon: An Evaluation*, 319.

61 "I think it rescued him": Dart, interview with author, September 13, 2007.

Oakley after Audubon

62 "Eliza Pirrie married," and related family history: *Oakley House Tour Manual*.

63 "Making the identical": *An Intimate Life of the American Woodsman*, 198–99.

63 After Lucretia's death: *Oakley House Tour Manual*.

65 she shared many of the artistic talents: Wilkie, *Creating Freedom*, 48.

65 "There can be no question": Bierce, letter to Ida Matthews, March 5, 1906.

66 "most treasured inhabitant": Porter, *The Collected Essays and Casual Writings of Katherine Anne Porter*, 168.

66 "the fruits of the earth": Ibid., 173.

67 "On the walls": Hoagland, *Heart's Desire*, 156–57.

67 "Time marches on": *On the Road with John James Audubon*, 257.

68 In 2006, builders broke ground: Sentell, "Audubon Bridge on Schedule; Price Tag Higher."

68 more than 150 species: "Birds of the Felicianas."

68 "not surpassed by any": *Birds of America* (online), http://www.audubon.org/bird/BoA/F26_G1j.html.

68 "extremely suspicious": Ibid., http://www.audubon.org/bird/BoA/F38_G1g.html.

68 "undulating curves": Ibid., http://www.audubon.org/bird/BoA/F8_G2g.html.

68 "The forest that he would see": Ouchley, interview with author, October 25, 2006.

69 "To my knowledge": Ibid.

69 "throughout the spring": Ibid.

69 drop in visitors: House, interview with author, September 30, 2006.

70 "none of them had ever heard": Anne B. Klein, interview with author, January 15, 2006.

71 "It was deteriorating": Ann Stirling Weller, interview with author, January 22, 2007.

Audubon's Oakley Legacy

71 "making the table": Woolf, *The London Scene*, 31.

71 "Some people stay": Elaine B. Smyth, e-mail message to author, December 11, 2006.

72 "Reproductions often look": Ibid.

72 "He is a true master": John O'Neill, e-mail message to author, October 30, 2006.

72 "Audubon wired up": Peterson and Peterson, eds., *Audubon's Birds of America*, introduction.

73 "Peru has been": O'Neill, "Studying and Painting Birds," in Dormon, ed., *Audubon: A Retrospective*, 94.

73 "the sweetest pleasures": *Writings and Drawings*, 128.

Bibliography

Abbey, Edward. *One Life at a Time, Please*. New York: Henry Holt, 1988.

American International Rattlesnake Museum, http://www.rattlesnakes.com/items/item09.html. Accessed January 12, 2007.

Arthur, Stanley Clisby. *Audubon: An Intimate Life of the American Woodsman*. New Orleans: Harmanson, 1937.

Audubon in Louisiana. New Orleans: Louisiana State Museum Friends of the Cabildo, 1966.

Audubon, John James. *The Birds of America* (online). Taken from 1840 first octavo edition. http://www.audubon.org/bird/BoA/BOA_index.html (accessed January 19, 2007).

———. *Mockingbirds and Rattlesnake*. American International Rattlesnake Museum Web site, http://www.rattlesnakes.com/items/item09.html (accessed January 12, 2007).

Audubon, Maria R., ed. *Audubon and His Journals*. Mineola: Dover, 1986.

Audubon in Louisiana. New Orleans: Louisiana State Museum Friends of the Cabildo, 1966.

Bierce, Ambrose. Letter to Ida Matthews, March 5, 1906, Audubon State Historic Site archives.

"Birds of the Felicianas." Baton Rouge: Louisiana Department of Culture, Recreation, and Tourism, 1993.

Blotner, Joseph. *Robert Penn Warren: A Biography*. New York: Random House, 1997.

Burt, John, ed. *The Collected Poems of Robert Penn Warren*. Baton Rouge: Louisiana State University Press, 1998.

Chalmers, John. *Audubon in Edinburgh and His Scottish Associates*. Edinburgh: NMS Publishing, 2003.

De Caro, Frank, and Rosan Augusta Jordan, eds. *Louisiana Sojourns: Travelers' Tales and Literary Journeys*. Baton Rouge: Louisiana State University Press, 1998.

DeLatte, Carolyn. *Lucy Audubon: A Biography.* 1982; rpr. Baton Rouge: Louisiana State University Press, 1998.

Dormon, James H., ed. *Audubon: A Retrospective.* Lafayette: Center for Louisiana Studies, 1990.

Durant, Mary, and Michael Harwood. *On the Road with John James Audubon.* New York: Dodd, Mead & Co., 1980.

Ford, Alice. *John James Audubon.* Norman: University of Oklahoma Press, 1964.

Hoagland, Edward. *Heart's Desire: The Best of Edward Hoagland: Essays from Twenty Years.* New York: Summit Books, 1988.

———. *Hoagland on Nature: Essays.* Guilford, Conn.: Lyons Press, 2003.

Irmscher, Christoph. "Audubon and the Veiled Lady." *American Scholar* 68 (Summer 1999), 65–76.

———. *The Poetics of Natural History: From John Bartram to William James.* New Brunswick, N.J.: Rutgers University Press, 1999.

———, ed. *John James Audubon: Writings and Drawings.* New York: Library of America, 1999.

La Fontaine, Jean de. *Selected Fables.* London: Penguin Books, 2006.

Louisiana State Museum. Standing Audubon exhibit, 660 North Fourth Street, Baton Rouge, La.

Marrs, Suzanne. *Eudora Welty: A Biography.* Orlando: Harcourt, 2005.

McClatchy, J. D., ed. *On Wings of Song: Poems about Birds.* New York: Knopf, 2000.

McCullough, David. Interview with author, March 1995.

Murphy, Robert Cushman. *John James Audubon (1785–1851): An Evaluation of the Man and His Work.* Speech originally published in the *New-York Historical Society Quarterly;* reprinted as a pamphlet by the National Audubon Society in October 1956.

Oakley House Tour Manual. Louisiana Department of Culture, Recreation, and Tourism, 2005.

Peterson, Roger Tory, and Virginia Marie Peterson. *Birds of Eastern and Central North America.* 5th ed. Boston: Houghton Mifflin, 2002.

———, eds. *Audubon's Birds of America: The Audubon Society Baby Elephant Folio.* New York: Artabras, 1981.

Porter, Katherine Anne. *The Collected Essays and Occasional Writings of Katherine Anne Porter.* Boston: Houghton Mifflin, 1970.

Rhodes, Richard. *John James Audubon: The Making of an American.* New York: Knopf, 2004.

———. *The Audubon Reader.* New York: Knopf, 2006.

Sanders, Scott Russell. *Audubon Reader: The Best Writings of John James Audubon.* Bloomington: Indiana University Press, 1986.

Sentell, Will. "Audubon Bridge on Schedule; Price Tag Higher." *The Advocate* (Baton Rouge), October 19, 2006.

Shaffer, Peter. *Lettice and Lovage: A Comedy in Three Acts.* London: Andre Deutsch, 1988.

Souder, William. *Under a Wild Sky: John James Audubon and the Making of "The Birds of America."* New York: North Point Press, 2004.

Streshinsky, Shirley. *Audubon: Life and Art in the American Wilderness.* New York: Villard Books, 1993.

Thoreau, Henry David. *A Week on the Concord and Merrimack Rivers; Walden, or, Life in the Woods; The Maine Woods; Cape Cod.* New York: Library of America, 1985.

Warren, Robert Penn. *The Collected Poems of Robert Penn Warren.* Baton Rouge: Louisiana State University Press, 1998.

Welty, Eudora. *The Eye of the Story: Selected Essays and Reviews.* New York: Vintage Books, 1979.

———. *A Writer's Eye: Collected Book Reviews.* Edited by Pearl Amelia McHaney. Jackson: University Press of Mississippi, 1994.

Wilkie, Laurie A. *Creating Freedom: Material Culture and African American Identity at Oakley Plantation, Louisiana, 1840–1950.* Baton Rouge: Louisiana State University Press, 2000.

Woolf, Virginia. *The London Scene: Six Essays on London Life.* New York: Ecco, 2006.

"Yellow Fever Deaths in New Orleans, 1817–1905." NUTRIAS, New Orleans Public Library Web site. http://nutrias.org/facts/feverdeaths.htm (accessed December 7, 2006).

A Note about Audubon's *Birds of America*

The LSU Libraries' Special Collections division is fortunate to possess not only a complete, bound copy of the magnificent double elephant folio first edition of Audubon's *Birds of America* (4 vols., London, 1827–1838) but also 120 separate plates, also from the first edition, which were given to the Libraries by a host of generous donors. Housed in Hill Memorial Library as part of the E. A. McIlhenny Natural History Collection, these holdings are augmented by a fine copy of the first octavo edition of *Birds*, published in the United States from 1840 to 1844.

The images reproduced in this book are derived both from the separate folio plates (when the Libraries had a separate plate) and from the octavo edition (when a separate double elephant folio plate was not available; because of the binding on the complete edition, its plates could not be reproduced). The folio and octavo editions differ in size and artistic medium. The double elephant folio, so called because of the size of the paper on which it was printed, measures approximately 40 inches by 27 inches and is made up of 435 aquatint engravings, in which the birds are depicted at life size. For the octavo edition, artists faithfully copied Audubon's original images to prepare smaller versions, suitable for printing in a book measuring approximately 11 inches by 7 inches. Audubon drew some of these smaller copies himself and also added some new species. In some cases he redrew plates, separating species that were depicted together in the folio, in order to accommodate the smaller size. Because of these additions, the octavo contains 500 plates, not all of which are copies of the folio plates. However, the octavo plates reproduced here all conform to the original folio images. Both editions were hand-colored with watercolors. Interested readers can learn more about the editions by consulting Waldemar Fries's *The Double Elephant Folio: The Story of Audubon's "Birds of America"* (Chicago: American Library Association, 1973) and Ron Tyler's *Audubon's Great National Work: The Royal Octavo Edition of "The Birds of America"* (Austin: University of Texas Press, 1993).

—Elaine B. Smyth
Head, Special Collections
LSU Libraries

The images for this book were created using digital technology. The separate plates were photographed by Adam Hess using a Sinar X with a Rodenstock Apo-Macro-Sironar lens and a Better Light digital scanning back. The octavo plates were digitized by Gina Costello, using an i2S DigiBook A1 10000RGB book scanner.

The LSU Libraries gratefully acknowledges the following donors of the elephant folio plates that are reproduced in this book:

Dr. and Mrs. O. J. Baker

Dr. and Mrs. Joseph W. Brouillette

Dr. and Mrs. John W. Chisholm

Dr.and Mrs. Arthur R. Colmer

Dr. and Mrs. Beverly J. Covington

Mr. and Mrs. Harold F. Dyson

Dr. George W. Fair

Dr. Fred H. Fenn

Dean and Mrs. Paul M. Hebert

Dr. and Mrs. Winston C. Hilton

Dr. and Mrs. Joseph H. Jones, Jr.

Dr. and Mrs. Arthur G. Keller

Dr. and Mrs. J. W. Kistler

Miss Sarah Lee

Dr. John Loos, Dr. J. Preston Moore, and Robert B. Holtman

Mr. and Mrs. Arthur M. Palmer

Mr. and Mrs. Malcolm G. Parker

Dr. and Mrs. Stanley W. Preston

Dr. and Mrs. Frank A. Rickey

Dean and Mrs. E. B. Robert

Mrs. Calvin Schwing

Dr. and Mrs. Hulen B. Williams